- THE DOCTOR IS IN -

DOCTOR

NerdLove

DATING ADVICE

FOR THE MODERN NERD

- SINCE 2011 -

SIMPLIFIED
Dating

The Ultimate Guide to Mastering The Art of Dating... Quickly.

Harris O'Malley

Other Books By Harris O'Malley

New Game + : A Geek's Guide to Love, Sex and Dating
When It Clicks: The Guide to Mastering Online Dating

Acknowledgements

To my friends the Sk8 Jesuits (VHive, yo!) who suggested that I needed to start actually writing a blog. To my friends Liz and Elise who patiently listened to me as I badgered them with question after question about the potential of ebooks and self-publishing. To Kira for being my proof-reader and of course my wife Cat for her patience, endurance, encouragement and willingness to put up with my crimes against grammar.

And to the men and women of the LEOG who helped make Dr. NerdLove happen in the first place.

Long Live The League.

Contents

ONE

INTRODUCTION

Our Story Thus Far...

Pardon me while I drop something painfully obvious on
you:

Dating is complicated.

Now, before you roll your eyes at me and start looking up
how to get a refund, let me explain where I'm going with
this.

Unlike many of my friends, I was not a "natural" when it
came to dating or knowing how to interact with women. In
fact, I was pretty much the furthest thing possible that you
could imagine.

I was, to put it mildly, a huge goddamn geek. I was
chubby, schlubby and pale, with the sort of skin tone that
can only be achieved by bathing in the cathode ray glow of
the TV while playing hours of Super Nintendo. I was into
comics back when comics were still the province of pimply
superhero fans or pretentious faux-intellectuals who wanted
to pretend that "graphic novels" were somehow different
than DC or Marvel's output. I was into anime and manga
when the only options available were dubious fan-subtitled
offerings that were third or fourth generation copies - this
was the days long before Sailor Moon or Pokémon

popularized the medium in the US. I was into computers, gaming consoles, fantasy novels... just about everything you could imagine that made vagina disappear like magic.

And oh boy did it ever.

Back in what I now call "the bad old days", I was just about every cliche you could imagine when it came to nerds trying to date. I spent so much time in The Friend Zone that I could declare it my primary residence and run for political office. I met my first "girlfriend" - in as much as you could call her that - on a glorified BBS system; we dated for less than two months before she cheated on me.

I'd never gotten past second base with her.

She was the last "girlfriend" - hell, the last date - I'd have for years

The majority of my love-life, before and since, had been a long and glorious tradition of being the classic Nice Guy - the insincere friend who did his best to trying to get girls to like him through what I call "The Platonic Best Friend Backdoor Gambit". I would be their bestest friend in the whole world, collecting "Nice Guy" tokens - bringing them soup when they were sick, buying them things they mentioned liking offhand, letting them cry on my shoulder whenever their asshole boyfriends would break their hearts - all in hopes that I could cash in those tokens and upgrade to "relationship"... or at least a couple nights of squishy noises.

It worked about as well as you might think - which is to say, not at all. In fact, I was far more likely to alienate my so-called friends by my actions; after all, I wasn't really their friend. If I was perfectly honest, then I was just pretending to be friends for as long as it took for me to get what I wanted. And really, who wants a friendship that's based on an agenda?

It wasn't until years later at my brother's wedding that I had what I refer to as my "Batman" moment. I had gone head to head with one of my oldest friends - a man who attracts women the way that cheese attracts mice - over a young woman and lost. Badly. As he was accompanying her back to her place, I was in my hotel room, alone, crying and masturbating out of frustration. In many ways, it was hitting rock bottom for me; I was determined that this could never happen to me ever again. The next day, I tripped over a copy of Neil Strauss' The Game at my local book-store... and it *blew my* ever-lovin' monkey mind. The idea that skill with women wasn't just *inborn,* but could be studied, *learned* like any *other* skill was a revelation to me. I took it as a sign. "Yes father," I vowed, "I will become... *a pick-up artist.*"

I spent *years* studying the intricacies of pick-up, fashion, seduction, sexology, social psychology, marketing and dating with the laser-like focus that only nerds and religious zealots can achieve. I studied people who were naturally gifted with women and people who'd *learned* how to improve themselves like I did. I read every book I could get my hand on and pushed myself far beyond what I had thought were my limits. I went out three or four nights a week minimum - approaching every woman I found vaguely attractive. I practiced pick-up lines, flirting, touching, teasing and fucking up every opportunity I could. I failed - *a lot* - and got shot down more times than I could count... *but* I was *learning.*

It wasn't the healthiest time of my life to be sure; when you're spending that much time doing little more than trying to teach yourself how to get women to sleep with you, you're going to be taking yourself to some dark places. I didn't like a lot of what the pick-up artist community had to say about women, and I *certainly* didn't like the person I found myself turning into. Eventually my path lead me away from a lot of those toxic beliefs and away from the pick-up community. I continued my self-directed education, finding ways of integrating what I'd learned with the man I *wanted* to be - someone who could be successful with women without being a noxious manipulator.

But it *was* an incredibly valuable experience. I learned more about myself and about social interactions than I'd ever known and pushed myself beyond what I would soon learn were my own self-limiting beliefs. I'd reinvented myself from the ground up. And I'd had a *lot* of fun doing it.

Especially when it came to dating.

I've lost track of how many people I've known who've told me they *hate* dating. They hate stress of trying to meet new people, the anxiety of planning the first date, the constant sense of uncertainty, the mind games, never knowing whether they're being *too* interested or *not interested enough...*

And to be honest, I thought they were crazy. Yeah, I'd been like that back in my bad old days, but dear God... after those years of study, dating to me was one of the greatest adventures imaginable. I loved the thrill of the chase, the intoxicating nervousness and manic energy that came from getting to know somebody new. The verbal sparring as we'd flirt back and forth, feeling each other out, the heady rush of sexual energy towards the end of the night when you knew you were standing on the precipice - would there be a good-night kiss, or might there be something *more* that night? It was a rush like no other for me.

For my friends though, dating was *exhausting*. It was a constant repetitive exercise of putting in massive amounts of effort for a minimal reward... if they didn't strike out entirely. They were hamsters on a wheel, running as fast and as hard as they could without actually *getting* anywhere while I was the one that would run as quick as possible before grabbing on to the rungs and hanging on for deal life and letting it whip me around like a demented carnival ride.

...

Yeah, sorry, that metaphor kind of got away from me.

The point is, they were spending most of their time and energy on the areas that would be the *least* productive and neglecting aspects where spending a little more time would produce huge results – small wonder they hated dating. To them, dating was a giant, confusing morass of conflicting information; the accepted narrative continually coming in conflict with reality as what we're *taught* seems to be completely at odds with how people act in real life.

The components of dating – where to meet people, how to approach a complete stranger versus somebody from your social circle, how to create sexual chemistry, how to engage someone emotionally, the myriad aspects of attraction, even something as simple as how to act on dates – can seem pants-shittingly intimidating. It's like asking someone to juggle knives while doing differential calculus in their heads at the same time. How are you supposed to keep all of this in mind, maintain an intelligent conversation with your date *and* still have a good time... never mind trying to secure that next date and and...

You see my point. It's the human equivalent of telling an artificial intelligence to divide by zero.

But it doesn't have to be.

The problem is that we as a culture treat being good with women as an inborn state; either you're just *naturally* adept at it or you're hopeless. You either just *get* dating on an unconscious level or you fumble your way through as best you can.

What we *don't* do is treat dating like a *skill*. And it's in treating it like a skill - no different from learning how to play an instrument, speaking a foreign language or playing a sport - that we can find the key to making dating *easier*.

One of the best ways to pick up a new skill is to, simply, break it down. Strip out the extraneous parts and just focus on the core. You can work outwards from there as you become more at ease.

So let's simplify dating a little, shall we?

Two

THE FUNDAMENTALS OF SIMPLIFIED DATING

Deconstructing Your Dating Life

I believe in efficiency when it comes to my social life –
especially to dating. I'm a firm believer that life is too short
and there's too much to do to waste time when you're
looking for a partner, whether it's for sex, companionship,
or romance. Over the years, I made a lot of mistakes that
ultimately meant I spent more time than I needed on
aspects of dating and personal development that didn't help
me nearly as much as I'd assumed; the results simply weren't
worth the initial level of investment that I put in.

Dating: I was doin' it wrong.

It took treating dating like a skill to help me realize just
how - and more importantly, where - I'd been wasting my
time.

Whenever we take on trying to learn new skill, we tend
to overwhelm ourselves by looking at the entire process as
though we had to master every single aspect of it.

Take learning a language, for example. You might look at
an English to Spanish dictionary and drive yourself
absolutely insane; how the hell are you supposed to
memorize all of that?

Except you don't have to. The key things you need to

learn in order to speak a language fluently - or at least with a high level of proficiency - are simple: the basic grammar and somewhere between 2,000 - 3,000 of the most common words. That's it. Those words formulate around 80% of all interactions in that language. Everything else is simply practice - preferably through immersion; you can be functionally fluent within half a year. You won't necessarily be writing poetry in Basque by that point, but you will be able to handle most of the every day conversations you might have - and have a much easier time learning the rest via context or continued study.

Similarly, if you want to learn how to play[1] a musical instrument, you can study musical theory and play scales until your fingers bleed... but if you learn four certain chord progressions, you can play damn near every pop or rock song ever written.

Then you have dating. Once you start approaching dating as a skill, it can seem absurdly daunting. Even regular readers of my blog take a look through the archives and start to wonder: "How am I supposed to learn all of this?" There's learning how to dress, how to flirt, looking for signs of interest, the many different ways of approaching somebody... and that's all before you've even gotten as far as asking them for their phone number, never mind gone out on a date with them. Then you get into even more complicated territory: how soon is too soon to call someone after you've gotten their number? Is it better to text or to call? Or maybe you should just add them on Facebook instead. Or is that too forward for someone you've just met?

It's enough to make you give up on dating all together. But it's that focus on every aspect that trips people up.

The key to mastering any skill quickly is to deconstruct it. You want to take it apart, strip it down to it's bare components and examine each part individually. Which parts are the most important? Which parts are the least important? Where do people screw up the most?

If you're familiar with business philosophy or the self-help industry, you may be familiar with the concept known as The Pareto Principle or the 80/20 rule. Named for the Italian economist Vilfredo Pareto who observed that 20% of the pea-pods in garden produced 80% of his peas... and then applied it to macro-economics; 20% of Italy's population, for example owned 80% of the land. The Pareto Principle has been applied to business (the ever popular 80% of your sales comes from 20% of your clients) to software (80% of software crashes are caused by the top 20% of recurring bugs in code) and in occupational safety (where 80% of the accidents and injuries suffered on the job come from 20% of the hazards).

And so in the name of efficiency, we want to take the same idea - that much of getting better at dating is identifying those areas where you get the most return on your metaphorical investment.

The Trouble With Dating

Traditional dating advice is, unfortunately, rife with wastes of time and energy. Much of the modern dating ritual - and ideas about what it takes to be successful with dating - is based less on reality and more on "well, this is how we've always done it". We take outdated gender roles and treat them as holy writ. We let fairy tales and fiction (and believe me, 99% of romantic comedy falls very firmly under the heading of "fairy tale") craft the narrative of how we're supposed to meet, mate, and settle down. We take dodgy pseudoscience and attempt to use it to retroactively justify our behavior as though the way we approach sex and relationships were biological destiny rather than social constructs.

Small wonder, then, that so many of us have no goddamn

idea what we're doing.

It's only natural that we're frustrated and looking for answers; all the conventional wisdom from the "just be yourself" to "be confident!" and "It'll happen when you least expect it" is less than useless. We're tired of constant failure, of being rejected over and over again, of first dates that don't lead anywhere and the feeling that love is something only other people get to experience. Even the magic bullets and emotional progression models of the seduction industry that promise that we'll be swimming in sex like Scrooge McDuck swimming through his money bin (and we'll pause to let that Cronenbergian mental image sink in) isn't the answer.

The problem is that we have all of these preconceived notions about dating. We tend to focus our attention on areas that we assume are hugely important because they fit our presuppositions and intellectual fallacies. We see women we're attracted to dating meat-heads, jocks, rich glamour boys and self-absorbed "masters of the universe" and assume that all women love assholes. We presume that attraction is based primarily on social status or physical looks when the reality is incredibly different.

At the same time, we neglect the areas that are important... because we're focused like a laser on trying to be "alpha" or crafting the perfect opening line. We spend hundreds of hours trying to get Brad Pitt's smile, Idris Elba's presence, Chris Hemsworth's leonine mane and Ryan Gosling's abs, but neglect the single most attractive aspect of a man... which isn't looks or money.

As a result: we've wasted a lot of time and energy, with very little to show for it. That's time and energy that we could have better spent on areas that would actually increase our chances of dating success, whether you define it as getting more casual sex, dating more women or finding that special someone (or someones) to settle down with.

To give a personal example: I spent a lot of time worrying

about how my perceived social value. At that point in my life, I was spending most of my time meeting women in bars and clubs as a pick-up artist. Just about every school of pick-up puts a great deal of importance on the idea of "social proof" - the idea that being a big-shot, the biggest swinging dick in the room, the man with all the connections and hook-ups is key in attracting women. Part of how this is expressed is to always be moving, always be talking to people (especially women - the better to inspire jealousy), befriending the bartender and the bouncers. If you can jump the line at the door, get free drinks from the bartender, meet and greet all of the big shots and VIPs by name... well, women's panties would just vaporize by being in your general vicinity.

In essence: I was trying to pull a Gatsby; be the guy everybody's talking about as soon as he walks through the door. And it was goddamned exhausting. I felt as though I had to be a social shark - if I stopped moving, everybody would notice and I'd start hemorrhaging value. I'd be that dork who was just holding up the bar, lost, alone and pants-shittingly terrified.

And then one day I came to the realization: nobody noticed. 99.999% of people couldn't care less about whether some stranger was talking to another stranger, no matter how handsome or well-dressed he was. Nobody gave a damn about whether I was alone or surrounded by people because they weren't paying attention to me at all. They were far more concerned with their immediate surroundings: the people they were talking to, whether they needed another drink, or even how much their shoes were just killing their feet.

I'd spent all of that effort trying to prevent a problem that didn't exist in the first place. Maximum effort but minimal return. It was one thing if I was at a bar where I was a legitimate regular and got the occasional buyback from the bartenders I'd befriended; that was part of who I was in my day to day life. It was quite another to try to force myself into being Mr. Life Of The Party when I would really rather just focus on the women I wanted to meet.

At the same time, I'd gotten bored of what I called my Standard First Date. It was a thing of glory, starting at an upscale bar not far from my house, moving to a bar nearby that always had live music, to a tapas restaurant then a hookah bar or a place I knew had decadent desserts before heading back to my place. By bouncing from place to place, it took advantage of a time-dialation effect that made it feel as though my date and I had known each other for far longer than we really had. And while I was having success with it (and the occasional "you take all your dates here, don't you?" Um... yup!) I could do it in my sleep. It was better than the bog-standard "dinner and a movie" but it was losing its charms and that was starting to affect the quality of the date.

So on a whim, I told my next date that we were going on a surprise date; I wasn't going to tell her where we were going, but she should dress to move and wear cute shoes. Our first date: going go-karting at an indoor track. We had a blast, with the friendly competition taking on a sexualized tinge as we would banter and talk smack between laps. She'd never had that much fun on a first date... and we ended up back at her place making out for hours. It recharged my social batteries and I was feeling a level of excitement and anticipation with future dates than I had in months.

In the process, I had also inadvertently stumbled on an aspect of dating and attraction that produced far more success than my previous efforts. The return - the awesome date, the sloppy make-outs, etc - greatly outstripped the effort put in.

(Don't worry, I'm going to tell you all about that aspect. Patience, young Jedi...)

So let's look at the key components of dating success...

and where guys waste the most time for no good reason.

---

[1] And I do mean "how to play", not "compose"; that's a different skill entirely.

Part One:

The Keys To Dating Success

THREE

SOCIAL CALIBRATION

"I Need to Make Some Calibrations..."

The first key to success in dating is learning social calibration.

The easiest way to describe social calibration is "the ability to correctly read and negotiate social situations". Social calibration means being able to read a person's social cues, respond to them appropriately. Being socially well-calibrated is key to being able to make people react in the way that you want them to, whether it's to put them at ease and make them comfortable or to make them excited or aroused. Someone who is socially well-calibrated is more at ease dealing with people because he or she understands what to expect from them and how to interact and influence with them.

It also means being able to find an individual's boundaries – the better to not cross them or to come as close as possible without going over them. A person who's socially calibrated also knows how to recover if he does end up causing offense or distress.

When you accidentally upset someone, how do you react? Do you smooth things over or do you try to explain why it's not fair for them to be upset? Are you able to keep your head, apologize and explain your intent, or do you freak out and end up making things worse?

Social calibration also means knowing what works for you. One mistake I see people make on a regular basis is trying to imitate someone without regard to how well that individual's style or personality meshes with their own, not realizing that what works for one person doesn't work for another. One of my friends - who has a natural gift for attracting women - is known for his outrageous and offensive sense of humor, which is part of his flirting style. He's an excellent example of perfect social calibration: he knows exactly where the line is and how to tip-toe up to it without going over. He may be making jokes that are downright offensive to a complete stranger but he will not only get her to laugh but also to appreciate him for being offensive because he knows his audience. He only wants women who would respond positively to his type of humor and knows how to screen for them... and his humor is part of his personality. If I were to try to say something similar to a woman then I'd likely end up getting a visit from the Slap Fairy.

Be Observant

Improving your social calibration demands that you become a more observant person. You need to become more in tune with other people's reactions and signals; the better you can read them, the better you can respond to them.

When it comes to dating, being able to read the body language and tonality of the person you're flirting with means that you're better able to tailor your interactions with them. Men and women have been socialized to communicate differently; men are taught to be much more direct and aggressive, while women are taught to be polite and deferential to others and to avoid giving offense if at all possible. Many times, women will stay in a conversation for far longer than they want to simply because they don't want to appear rude and can't find a socially acceptable way of exiting the situation; meanwhile, the men appear clueless at her distress because they're focusing on the macro - she's still talking to you, she's laughing at your jokes - and ignoring the micro - the way her eyes dart around the room or the way that her laugh has a brittle, uncomfortable quality.

It's these subtle cues that shape the interaction; the better you become at picking them up, the better your calibration.

Fortunately, most signs aren't all that subtle or hard to read; you just have to be looking for them.

Imagine that you're having a conversation with a woman you're attracted to. How is she reacting? Is she keeping her attention focused on you, or are her eyes starting to flit around the room? When someone is attracted to you, they're going to give you their full attention. If she seems distracted, then she's signaling to you that she's uninterested in what you have to say and isn't paying attention. If she's looking around the room, she's trying to make eye-contact with a friend to let them know that she needs an escape-hatch. If she checks her watch repeatedly, she's quite literally counting down the minutes until she can say "I've got to go talk to someone else."

Is she relaxed or starting to shift her weight from one foot to the other? These little signs let you know whether she's interested in what you have to say or whether she's getting ready to walk away. What about her body? Is she mirroring your posture and body-language? That's a sign that she's interested in you. Closed off body language, on the other hand - crossed arms, angling her body away from you - is a sign that you make her uncomfortable. If she's laughing, is it a full-throated laugh or polite and brittle? If she's smiling at you, is it a polite smile or does it reach up to her eyes, causing the crinkling at the edges?

If you touch her, does she tense up or does she relax into your touch? When you take your hand away, does she respond by touching you?

Being able to notice these little signs and tells are not only how we tell whether the person you're talking to is into you, but also part of how to avoid being creepy by accident; people will let you know through their body language that you're toeing the line far before you cross it.

Understanding The Context

Part of how we avoid awkwardness - or being seen as a creeper - is to be able to read the context of the situation and adapt to it. It's a means of displaying that, yes, we understand the implied social contract and are willing to follow it.

Context ultimately colors how we interpret everything; telling a raunchy joke at a rowdy bar is socially acceptable. Telling the exact same joke at a Catholic baptism, on the other hand, is not. If I were to approach a woman on a quiet street downtown in the middle of the day and ask her for the time or directions to Mr. Noodle, my actions would be seen as normal for that time and place. If I approached that same woman on the same street in the middle of the night - again, just asking for the time or directions to a local restaurant - the context will be completely different and that will color how she sees me. I'm now not engaging in a simple request, I'm a potential threat to her personal safety and need to be judged accordingly.

The social context of a situation dictates the expectations of the participants and thus affects the rules of what's socially acceptable. A nightclub, for example, has a specific kind of atmosphere; people go there dressed to impress, grind on the dance floor and hook up with strangers. You can get away with being more overtly sexual in your flirting in a club than you could at Starbucks.

Similarly, many bars are considered locations where it is not only socially acceptable to meet people but is considered to be a part of the social contract; if someone is at a bar that caters to a more socially active crowd – a DJ, open floorspace for mingling, mixed drink specials – it can generally be assumed that they are open to meeting new people.

On the other hand, a bookstore is a calm, soothing place; not necessarily a place where strangers try to pick one another up.[1]

Trying to approach a woman browsing the mystery section of Barnes and Noble the same way you would approach her at a rowdy singles bar is going to make her uncomfortable at best and probably get you thrown out by the staff; it's completely out of keeping with the accepted social context. In a club, you're expected to be more energetic and outgoing; in a bookstore, maintaining that same level of energy would make you seem as though you did too much crank and just finished disassembling your stereo. Being as overtly touchy-feely at a bookstore as you might be at a nightclub is a great way to get maced.

Incongruence

Congruence is the property of being suitable or in harmony with the circumstance or situation, and it's a key aspect of respecting the social context. When you're being incongruent, you're not fitting in, either with event, the location or who you're presenting yourself as. Behavior, clothing, body language, even your persona can all be ways of being incongruent... and it will make people uncomfortable.

For example: consider the way you dress. How you dress is how you present yourself; our clothes, in many ways, are a visible indicator of who we consider ourselves to be. If you see someone in a smart, well-tailored three-piece suit, you automatically make certain assumptions about who they are and what they do - odds are that they're in business and relatively financially affluent. Similarly, if we see someone in a ripped up concert tee, jeans, a leather jacket covered in studs and patches, and Chuck Taylors, we're going to assume that they're likely in the punk scene.

But when that guy with the massive Misfits logo safety-pinned on the back of his jacket starts talking about making being part of a venture capital firm... well, we're probably going to assume that they're either lying or pretending to be a punk for some reason. Similarly, if you're dressed like a banker and telling someone about how you love restoring Harley-Davidson panheads, you're going to leave people feeling confused; you may be telling the truth, but what you're saying is completely seems utterly out of character for the way you're presenting yourself.

This isn't to say that you can't have wide and varied interests. It's not impossible - vanishingly unlikely but not impossible - to find a stock-broker sporting a Black Flag tattoo and jamming out to The Damned. But it's going to be a speed-bump in their attraction to you. It's one thing to have layers; it's another when you're night-and-day different from who you appear to be.

Behavior is another way of being incongruent. If you're coming up to someone at Whole Foods with the same bouncy energy that you might have if you were at a club to hear your favorite band, you're going to seem incredibly off. You'll be incongruent with the location and the unspoken rules that govern the location and your interaction. She's going to be wondering just what's wrong with you rather than finding you charming and delightful.

To take it in another direction: you may be telling her about all the fun you had at South By Southwest, but your body-language is completely at odds with what you're saying. Your story about how you bluffed your way backstage says you're trying to show her that you're an outgoing, adventurous person with oodles of confidence but your hunched-over, shifty body language is saying that you're nervous and have low self-esteem. It may have actually happened, but when your mouth is saying completely different things from your body, people will naturally assume you're lying. It's simply not congruent with who you seem to be.

Being incongruent is a sign of poor calibration. It tells people that you aren't attuned to the social dynamics of the situation, whether it be the situation or your identity.

But What If You Screw Up?

This is the part that often paralyzes people: the fear of fucking up. They have visions of being exiled from their social circle, of having to leave their class or their gaming group in shame... As a result, they often freeze up rather than risk talking to someone or flirting with them and making a mistake. But shit happens and we're all human; even the best of intentions can mean occasionally tripping over your dick or slamming your foot in your mouth at record speed.

And? So what if you do? What if you end up creeping someone out? Or insulting them? Or commit any of the death-by-a-thousand-cuts mistakes that kill a social interaction?

The answer is very simple: you apologize, you take a step back (sometimes literally) and you move on to something else. Most people will take your apology at face value and be willing to forgive and forget, provided you ensure that you don't make that mistake again. Continuing to dwell on it - constantly apologizing, being unwilling to let it go - is only going to make things worse by constantly drawing attention to your faux-pas instead of just acknowledging that you just had an awkward moment.

If you've somehow committed some huge and unforgivable transgression, then you apologize, cut your losses and go.

Congratulations: you just had a learning moment. So learn from it. But don't let it destroy you.

Just because you fucked up somehow doesn't automatically mean that you've failed and you're being entered into the Undatable Creepers registry. It just means you made a mistake and the sooner you get over the idea that one mistake is instantly fatal to attraction, the more relaxed you will be. Not every mistake is an unrecoverable, game-ending disaster; a sincere apology can make the difference between being able to salvage the situation and having to give up and try again with someone else.

And you may well find that it's in pulling out from a downward spiral that you learn the most.

There's a saying in pick-up circles that's fitting: the first thousand rejections don't count. Those first thousand rejections aren't about you, they're part of the learning process; they're no different then all the wrong notes when you're studying guitar or every missed shot when you're practicing free-throws. Before you work through those first thousand rejections you're not even in the game yet; you're still building up the skill-set that will mean you get rejected less and less as you improve.

The better calibrated you are, the better you are at understanding and fitting in with the social dynamics. Being better socially calibrated means you're not giving a creepy vibe or saying the wrong things, and *that* means you're able to spend more time finding the person that's right for you.

-----

[1] Although it *can* be great place to meet women,

especially if you're interested in geeks...

FOUR

CHEMISTRY

What Is Chemistry?

The next key aspect of successful, simplified dating is chemistry.

Chemistry has a tendency to be defined as an ineffable part of dating. Everyone agrees that chemistry is important, but the moment you ask them to describe it and you'll end up with a mix of inconclusive - and unhelpful - answers. "It's... you know. That spark." "That feeling." "That moment when the two of you just... click.

Frankly, you'd have more success asking nerds to explain why the Fantastic Four's costumes don't burn or tear whenever they use their powers[1]. You'll get the same number of buzzwords and it'll be just as helpful.

This, sadly, is what happens when you ask people to explain emotions; humans are good at understanding that we feel a particular way, but we have a damned hard time understanding *why*. More often than not, we backfill the reasons for the way we feel in ways that make sense to us later. And that leads us to the problem with the way we view chemistry.

To make it almost reductively simple, chemistry is a mix of emotional engagement and sexual attraction.

Because we have such a hard time explaining chemistry, it takes on the level of myth; it becomes an aspect of fate rather than a matter of sexual and emotional compatibility. It becomes another form of "love at first sight" or "finding your soulmate". It's either there or it isn't and is only found via random chance.

Of course, I imagine you can already guess what I'm about to tell you. Chemistry isn't a matter of random chance - it's something that you can make happen, provided that you know what you're doing.

The key to chemistry is to remember that you need balance. Yes, it's tempting to focus all of your attention on building sexual attraction - especially if you're looking for sex partners rather than a romantic relationship. Physical desire is all well and good, but for true chemistry, you need more than just sex. Even when you're burning up the sheets every night and twice on Sundays, the hottest of relationships can be brought down if the two of you simply can't hold a conversation or agree on what to watch on Netflix. "Hot and dumb" *does* have its appeal for both genders, but most people are looking for more than just animal attraction. They also want to feel that they connect with someone on an emotional and intellectual level.

In other words: you're not just trying to get into their pants; you're trying to get into their *heads*.

Sexual Tension

Sexual tension is one of the cornerstones of chemistry. Not sexual *attraction*, mind you; it's possible to think someone's hot but want to bang them. You want sexual *tension*. Sexual tension is desire for someone that is unfulfillable, whether by circumstance, obstacles... or by design.

One of the most common denominators of humanity is that we almost instinctually want the things we can't have.

The easiest way to make somebody want something is keep it from them. It gets even worse when it's *just* out of our reach. Think of it like a kitten and a length of string. When it's just laying there, they're not interested. But when you jerk it away from them... well, that's when they pounce on it. Hang it just outside of their reach and they'll *leap* for it.

When your desire for something is frustrated, you tend to want it more. The closer you get to getting it, but without actually being able to achieve it causes the desire to grow. Check eBay the morning after a new iPhone is released; the site gets flooded with listings for brand new iPhones going for hundreds of dollars over MSRP... and people snatch them up simply because they couldn't get one as soon as they wanted.

But it's more than just waving something in somebody's face and saying "Hey, you can't have this." After all, if someone barely knows you, they're not going to be that invested in trying to land you. You need to build anticipation.

Think about roller-coasters. What makes them work isn't the steep drops, the loops and corkscrews, it's the long build-up at the beginning. It's the building of expectations that makes the sudden drop immediately afterwards so amazing; just launching into the ride – the way some coasters do – is less satisfying.

Now think of the best kisses - the ones where you *know* it's going to happen, when the desire to kiss is so palpable that you could cut it with a knife. They're the ones where you move in slowly, ever so slowly, while your heart pounding so loudly you're amazed that the neighbors aren't calling to complain, when every nerve-ending seems to be on fire... and then that little frisson of sexual energy right before your lips meet.

Now imagine the other pulling away at the very last moment.

Suddenly that kiss is the most important thing in the

universe.

Sexual tension – deliberately building and then frustrating sexual interest – is all about the lead-up, the build up and then the release. It's a game of "come here, now go away", where you run hot and cold – you pull someone in, then push them away. You start to build the tension and then cut it off. Think of it like a pressurized tank of gas: it has an emergency release valve. If the pressure grows past a certain point, the tank ruptures; the valve is there to equalize the pressure, keeping it just below the danger zone.

It's the same with building sexual tension: keep building the tension for too long, whether through flirting or physical contact, and you're going to redline – either you'll creep out your date or overwhelm them. Either way, the moment is over and you're stuck in recovery mode instead of leading towards a night of passion and several hours of squishy noises back at your place. You want to provide an out, a release in order to pull the tension back. Suddenly taking the tension away actually works to your favor by creating a vacuum. The tension becomes even more desirable by its absence. Now that it's gone, the other person to want to feel it again. Push, then pull. Bait, then release. The uncertainty, keeps everyone on their toes and longing for that build up and final release.

Find Your Passion

If you want to connect with someone, you need to find your passion. Passion is magnetic. Passion is provoking. Passion is one of the most attractive aspects somebody can have... and it will draw people to you.

We gravitate towards people with passion because they have a level of confidence and self-assuredness that comes with loving something without giving a damn about what other people think. It's invigorating;   they're just so exuberant and alive when they talk about the things they love that it's hard not to feel swept up in their emotion. Even when it's something painfully boring, being able to express your love for it can make it compelling.

Tom Cruise is my go-to example when it comes to expressing passion. Whether you love him or think he's a nut-job, you can't deny that when he's on, he's electric. He is absolutely *riveting*, whether he's super-spy Ethan Hunt or super-agent Jerry McGuire. He can deliver a soliloquy on the wonders of something as mundane as traffic patterns and make it just as exciting and emotional as promising an up-and-coming athlete that he will *personally* see to it that they will be starring in their own video game and designing a brand of shoes with their name on it that's advertised during the Super Bowl. And when someone gets caught up in that excitement and starts to bounce up and down *with* him, you're right there too because god*damn* if you aren't feeling it too.

People with passion in their lives have a certainty and assuredness about them because they love what they're passionate about whole-heartedly. They don't worry about "maybe I shouldn't get this excited over my favorite bands" or "maybe I should act my age instead of waxing rhapsodic about the power that books have over me." They just *go* for it. That willingness to embrace something without worrying about how it looks or whether it's "cool" or not is refreshing... and all too rare.

Having passion in your life is part of what makes you come alive and separates you from the people who just exist. We live in a society where people are disconnected from their interests and which disdains exuberance or loving things with abandon. Too many people are content to simply exist, following a routine of "wake up, eat, work, eat, sleep, repeat" day in and day out, living out Thoreau's "lives of quiet desperation". People with passion in their lives are driven. They don't just meander or float through life, they have purpose. They have something they live for, something they care about with an intensity that you just don't see often. There's a part of their life that brings them fulfillment, that pushes them on and inspires them.

Even if it's not a passion that you both share, when you feel passionate about something and you can communicate that passion to other people, they can't help but feel connected to it.

Flirting, Teasing and Sexual Humor

Flirting is a key point of sexual tension... and it's something of a lost art. All too often, attempts at flirting either turn into paying too many compliments (and ending up looking desperate), telling jokes (and ending up looking like you're practicing your stand-up routine) or just "negging" or using insults as a way of either showing you're not intimidated by them or trying to make them seek your approval (and thus, looking like an asshole).

Flirting is, at its core, a way to engage, size up and generate attraction in a prospective mate. It's light and it's friendly. It's a combination of banter, body language and teasing.

You need to find your own flirting style; some people prefer to use body language. Some people will do mini-roleplays, conveying some future adventure together. Personally, I'm a fan of teasing as a part of flirting. Teasing is the art of telling someone you like them while saying something mean in a playful way. The antagonistic aspect of teasing follows the push-pull dynamic of sexual tension; you're giving a compliment (the push) and putting up a barrier or disqualification at the same time (the pull).

"You're the most awesome person I've met... so far."

"Dude, you're hilarious... it's too bad you're such a dork."

When done properly, it invites someone to zing you back instead of getting offended. For example – taken from my personal experience: "Oh, I'm the dork? I didn't realize someone wearing a Star Wars tee-shirt[2] was allowed to cast judgement on somebody else."

When you write it out, this exchange can seem like two people insulting each other. In fact, you could be forgiven for assuming that this was going to end with two very annoyed people. However, when you factor in outside elements: our tone of voice, sitting together at the bar, her knee up against my thigh, her smiling and delivering a playful punch when she said it – it's not an insult match, it's banter. It's closer to a sword-fight[3] between two masters. It's about creating sparks with each pass rather than hurting each other's feelings.

The subtext of the conversation – beyond the fun that was to be had by gently digging at one another – was simple. I was saying "I like you and I know you like me already, so I want to make you work for this." She was responding with "I know exactly what you're doing and I'm going to volley it right back to you. Let's see if you can keep this up."

In practice, you want to cut the conversational thread and move on to another topic – one unrelated to what you were just discussing and one that doesn't immediately lead to *another* verbal fencing match. You need to space things out, to give the tension room to grow. Going from banter to banter to banter can be exhausting emotionally; you end up feeling as though you're constantly having to be on your guard rather than letting yourself relax and enjoy each other's company.

One critical aspect is that your flirting should have a slight sexual edge to it. After all, you do want to establish early on that you're interested in them as a potential love interest - or at least a good time - rather than just a platonic friend. Trying to hide that side of you only serves to tell her that you're not attracted to her sexually.

That being said, you don't want to be crude or blunt either; that's a very good way to kill her interest and display low social calibration. You want to use humor and playfulness to bring it up in a way that's not threatening or creepy – and, if need be, can be dialed back if you make her uncomfortable. Calling her naughty, portraying her as a sexual predator, implying that she's trying to get you drunk to take advantage of you or that you know that girls like her have only one thing on their minds... these are all teasing aways to interject a slight sexual edge. You will want to ask qualifying questions regarding sex and that have a sexual edge to them: "What are you passionate about?" is a good one, as is "What really drives you wild?"

Ideally, you want to be charming and just a little edgy. If you find you're making her uncomfortable, you need to apologize and dial it back... immediately.

Interested is Interesting

Want to get someone interested in you? Show them that you find them fascinating.

It may seem self-involved, but we instinctively like people who show that they like *us*. We like to think that we're all special snowflakes with a rich inner core of wonder and beauty, just waiting for other people to discover it. Other people letting us know that they think we're cool and are interested in what we have to say validates our belief that we are, in fact, awesome. It's an incredible feeling.

This isn't to say that the path to a person's heart is by shoving your nose as far as possible up their rectum; being a suck-up isn't going to get you far with anyone who isn't holding open auditions for the role of "toady". It screams of neediness and desperation, which is the Anti-Sex Equation. Most people don't want an ass-kisser, and those that do... well, they're best avoided anyway. Instead, you want to make a point of showing how interested you are by being an active listener.

There are two types of people in the world: people who actively listen and people who wait for their turn to talk. Active listening in a conversation means that you're not just hearing what she's saying; it shows that you're actually giving her your full attention instead of getting distracted by your own thoughts or letting your mind wander while you wait for her to finish up. Most conversations tend to be profoundly one-sided: one person talking, with the other making occasional monosyllabic "yes, I'm still listening" noises while they wait for their opportunity to talk. Active listening, on the other hand, means not just paying attention to what your date has to say, but making a point of engaging them – making sure that you understand and asking questions in order to prompt them to expand upon the topic.

That asking questions part, by the way, is critical. To start with, when someone is asking a lot of questions, they're showing that they're interested in what you have to say... and by the same token, they're interested in *you*. By taking part in the topic rather than passively sitting there absorbing what she has to say like a conversational sponge, you're saying that you think they're worth listening to. It doesn't even have to be terribly complicated; studies have found that simply repeating the last few words as a question helps build rapport. Obviously you don't want to do this with everything they *say*, but it's an easy go-to when you find yourself stuck for an idea; it's a verbal sign that you're paying attention and that you're engaging with them.

One of my best friends networks the way other people breathe and can make friends with just about anyone. Her trick is that she immediately shows that she's interested in hearing what they have to say about any topic that comes up by asking questions, then using *those* answers as a springboard to getting deeper into what they think. She makes a point to relate to them, pointing out how their experiences or interests intertwine or contrast, and then moves on to asking about *another* conversational subject. Repeat the process a few times and she comes away with a valuable new contact who thinks she's a cool person to know.

You've Got To Touch

Touch is one of the most important - and under-utilized - parts of building chemistry. The power that touch has in generating sexual tension cannot be understated. Physical contact is a key component to sexual arousal; call it one of the benefits of those thousands of nerve-endings we have running through our skin.

Now to be sure, you need a certain level of intimacy and comfort before you can move from casual touching to more sexually charged touch – you don't want to reach up and stroke the neck of the woman you just met at the bar unless you're interested in wearing an amaretto sour for the rest of the night.

You need to understand the intimacy ladder when it comes to touching: the upper arm is the least intimate, followed by the forearm, the hand, the knee, the thigh, the neck and the face.

Hopefully it should be obvious why "breasts" aren't on the list.

Different women have very differing levels of comfort with a relative stranger touching them; some people are very touchy-feely and others are emphatically not. Thus, you need to take care to not freak her out or offend her. When you're trying to break the touch-barrier, you want to start with the least-intimate and manner of making contact: touch her on the forearm or on the upper arm with the back of your hand when you emphasize a point when you talk to her. It's non-threatening and socially acceptable - especially when flirting or on a date.

Pay attention to how she reacts. Does she stiffen up, even slightly? She's not ready for you to be making contact. Take a step back and spend more time flirting; she will make it clear through body language and proximity whether or not she is more comfortable with your touching her.

If she doesn't indicate that she's uncomfortable, you may want to move from there to offering a high-five when she tells an awesome story. A knee up against her knee when you're sitting next to each other is subtle but powerful; if she doesn't pull her knee away, it's a sign that she's possibly interested in more intimate contact later on.

Don't ignore the back or hips either. A hand on the small of the back, guiding your date through the restaurant or to your car can be quite the turn on, as can physically turning her by her hips. One of the reasons why latin dances such as salsa, cha-cha and meringue are so charged is because of the way that the leading partner guides the following partner by physically moving her hips.

One popular trick I've learned – and used with great success – from player friends of mine is what's known as the "almost-kiss". It's a little cheesy and fairly obvious, but it's also incredibly fun. You want to try this when you're having a more active, playful date; this isn't something you want to attempt when you're at a quiet wine-bar. There're many variations of this; some people will set it up by suggesting that you try an almost-kiss, but swear that you're not going to actually kiss because it's just too soon. You lean in close as though for a kiss and hover close to their lips for a moment or two and then pull back – the push-pull dynamic in action, building up the sexual tension then pulling back just as you're starting to get near the point of no return. It can take some practice – if you're not careful, the set-up is going to sound cheesy, and not in a charming way – but it's a powerful technique.

As things progress and the two of you are becoming more comfortable and into each other, you might run your fingertips gently down their back before pulling back and stepping aside. Warm breath on the neck – perhaps accompanied by "you smell nice" can make the difference between a chaste kiss and being grabbed by the back of your favorite head for major make-outs. The hair can also be an incredibly charged area; stroking the hair, or even running your fingers through it and grasping it gently near the scalp can help charge things up.

Remember, you want to maintain the push-pull dynamic. For every two steps forward – kissing, say – you want to pull back again. "That's all you get for now," you might say, after a particularly passionate kiss, pulling yourself away and keeping a physical distance between you. It may seem counter-intuitive – if you're kissing, you would think you would want to try to move things forward, not backwards – but showing restraint, taking the tension to a crescendo and leaving it there dials the sexual tension way up. It's a powerful move... and it's better to leave them wanting more than pushing too far and risk blowing the whole thing.

Make Her Feel

Part of what makes for good chemistry is to affect someone on an emotional level. We've all been on dates where the strongest emotion we felt was boredom and we were hoping that somebody would crash their car through the window if only so something interesting would happen. The worst dates aren't the ones where you actively dislike someone or things go horribly wrong... after all, at least then you're feeling something, even if it's anger, fear or sheer mindless panic.

No, the worst dates, the ones that make you want to give up on dating altogether, the ones where you don't feel anything and you've just watched precious hours of your life whither away and die before your eyes.

It's all well and good to be able to engage someone intellectually, but you need to spur an emotional reaction as well. Of course, getting an emotional reaction is dead simple; act like a giant cock and you'll almost certainly get a reaction. Of course, you'll also likely end up getting slapped, cursed out and have pastries thrown at you, but at least it was a reaction… *right?*

Yeah. Not so much.

You want to elicit emotions from your dates; we appreciate people who can make us feel excitement, curiosity or the warm-and-fuzzies.

Getting the reactions you want on the other hand: laughter, excitement, "that's interesting" or "awwww" are tougher. One of the best ways of taking your date on an emotional journey is through telling stories. Stories are incredible tools when it comes to dating – they keep people entertained, they are a chance to show how awesome your life is without appearing conceited and, critically, when done right, they make people feel. You capture their interest and lead them on an emotional journey while conveying who you are as a person.

It's easy to make an opportunity to tell some stories about yourself; if you've already been making a point to ask questions, you can use those as a springboard to set up information about yourself. If you're talking about traveling, you have an opportunity to transition into a story about something cool that happened to you the last time you travelled. Don't have any cool traveling stories? Pick an aspect of travel and relate that to a different area of your life.

Just remember: brevity is the soul of wit and a long story

is the death of the attention span. You don't want to let your stories drag on. The longer you talk, the more likely it will be that you're going to lose their interest. Keep your stories short and to the point; if your story is taking longer than a couple of minutes, it's too long. You need to edit the fuck out of them and cut away the fat. If you need to, write them out in advance and just start trimming bits until you have something that works.

---

[1] Yeah, yeah, "unstable molecules". This is about as helpful as "reverse the polarity flow off the main reflector dish".

[2] For the record, that shirt was a vintage import from Japan and it was *awesome*, dammit.

[3] "…how appropriate, you fight like a cow."

FIVE

AN ATTRACTIVE LIFESTYLE

You Are Not Your Job, Your Apartment or your Fucking Khakis

Consider your day to day existence. You do have more to your life than just trying to get laid, right? You don't just live a never-ending cycle of "get up, go to work, eat, go home, go to bed", do you? You have hobbies. You have interests. Right?

You *should*, because it affects far more than you'd think. How we see and interact with the world is colored and filtered by our day-to-day behaviors and activities; what we do every day wears a groove into our brains that affects everything we do and see... not to mention affecting the people we meet and the way they perceive us.

A person's lifestyle is often the single most neglected area of self-improvement, especially when you're trying to get better at dating. Small wonder why: it's effectively the most invisible part of a person. When we think of an "attractive lifestyle", we don't think of the basics: what you do (besides your job), what your interests are, how you pursue your passions. We tend to focus on the parts we can show off like a particularly insecure peacock. The lion's share of attention is showered on surface issues – physical attractiveness, having witty opening lines, being able to flirt and banter – because they're so much more *visible*. We see the good looking guy making women laugh and we want to be like him. We see Bond charming women effortlessly and we wish we had that sort of charisma. As a result: we focus on the flash and smoke at the expense of the deeper issues.

One of the most common mistakes that people make when talking about lifestyle is that they equate a "good" lifestyle with material goods and success. It's a truism in many PUA circles, for example, that to have an attractive lifestyle means a flashy car, the most stylish clothes or a socially desirable job – all the better to rope in those women who "only" date rich guys / alphas / what have you. And yet for all that people will claim that being financially well off is a pre-requisite for dating success, I have known plenty of people who are richer than God who can't score a date to save their lives. Just the simple state of having loads of cash doesn't automatically guarantee a happy or successful romantic life; just like being physically attractive doesn't automatically mean that you're going to be deluged in girlfriends. Lifestyle is more than just superficial issues such as job, income and spending levels, and fashion choices. Your lifestyle is the manner in which you live, which reflects who you are as a person. It includes your values and your attitudes, what you find fulfilling and where you choose to spend your time and attention – and this, in turn, will affect how you present yourself and how you come across to others.

While financial success can bring comfort and increase one's opportunities in other areas, it is by no means the definition of a "good" or "attractive" lifestyle. You can have money or a high-status job and still have little to no satisfaction with your life. Lifestyle isn't just about what you own or the size of your apartment – it's about how you live your life, how you pursue your passions, how you spend your time and who you spend it with.

This isn't to say that you must have your dream job or make buckets of money before you can start dating; it means that you need to have something in your life that brings you satisfaction and fulfillment.

Most writers or artists for example, have jobs that they don't care for because being a full-time writer or artist usually doesn't pay the bills. Their day job may not bring much in the way of personal satisfaction, but it does give them the opportunity to indulge their passion: painting, music, writing, etc. Being able to follow their passion – even though it may not bring financial success – helps enhance their lifestyle.

If you aren't happy with your lifestyle – you work a job you hate for far too little money, you have no creative outlet, you're socially disconnected, or you have little to your life beyond just day to day drudgery – you are going to have a much harder time meeting people and finding people who want to spend time with you. Your dissatisfaction will affect how you interact with the world around you and how others react to you. The less you have going for you that makes you happy, the more problems you will face in your dating life.

Part of an attractive lifestyle is pursuing your interests and your passions, finding the things that bring you joy and satisfaction. Having passion in your life is an incredibly attractive trait and exploring and expanding your horizons helps make you a more well-rounded, interesting individual. This is why it's important to cultivate your interests and hobbies, especially if they are in areas you've always wanted to explore but have been afraid to; taking chances and facing your fears are great ways of building confidence on top of improving your lifestyle.

Your Lifestyle Is Your Filter

Part of why your lifestyle is important is in how it affects the people you meet and the people who will be attracted to you.

Imagine a life where you're always meeting incredible, attractive, awesome people: not just women or potential romantic partners but future business contacts, networking opportunities and lifelong friends. They just naturally enter your life, instead of having to go and seek them out.

How wonderful would it be if the woman (or man, or what-have-you) of your dreams just became part of your everyday life instead of having to go out searching for them?

Pretty awesome, right?

This is why your lifestyle is a critical cornerstone of dating.

Not everyone is cut out for - or interested in - hitting the bars and clubs to get laid or find a relationship. For many, the act of deliberately seeking out a girlfriend, even in as neutral and comfortable a space as a coffee shop or a bookstore, is so out of character as to be laughable… so how are they supposed to find love?

And the answer is "through their lifestyle".

One of the reasons I constantly advocate exploring hobbies and being more social is that it makes meeting new people a natural and inevitable part of your life. Instead of having to go out specifically to find people, an active and engaging lifestyle helps bring the people you are interested in to you. Going out and leading an active life helps to put you in a position where meeting new people is going to just happen. If your lifestyle is predominantly one of staying at home and cutting yourself off from contact with the world, you are going to have a much harder time meeting people than someone going out and taking some language classes or participating in an amateur sports league. [1]

Similarly, having an attractive lifestyle will increase your personal appeal to others – if you're leading an interesting life, others are going to want to be a part of it. On the other hand, if your day-to-day existence consists of shuttling between work and home with only a few rounds of Call of Duty to break up the hours in between getting home and passing into unconsciousness, far fewer people are going to want to take part. People who dig that do exist... but they're going to be fewer and farther between, and you'll need to adjust your expectations accordingly.

Your lifestyle will also help determine the type of people you meet and attract. Despite what Paula Abdul told us, opposites *rarely* attract; we are much more likely to be interested in people who are similar to us. If there's a particular type of person you're interested in – alt-girls, for example – then you are much more likely to find success if you are compatible and congruent with their world.

A 56 year old corporate type who's into opera and wine-tastings isn't necessarily going to be attractive to the 23 year old recent college graduate in a retail job who lives for shot specials downtown and clubbing on weekends, no matter how much the corporate type may want it. Their lifestyles are going to be too incompatible; they have entirely different life experiences, values, attitudes and priorities. The business type rarely succeeds with the bohemian; more often than not their lifestyles conflict with one another to a point where it's almost impossible for the two to be happy together. The more overlap between lifestyles that you have, the more basis for attraction and commonalities exist.

If you're an introvert, the odds of meeting someone that you're interested in – and who would be interested in you – at a Thirsty Thursday happy hour at Baby A's are remote at best.

This is not to say that nerds can and should only date nerds, mind you, or that introverts can only date introverts. You don't need matching lifestyles so much as compatible ones. A geek who's a bit of a homebody with an interest in anime and video games can still find happiness with a non-geek who also enjoys quiet nights at home shotgunning episodes of **Orange Is The New Black** on Netflix, but they will be far less happy with an outdoors-y extrovert who doesn't care for reading and prefers bar-hopping to a night in.

Play To Your Strengths

One of the common mistakes I see when people talk about what makes an attractive lifestyle is the assumption that there is one lifestyle that is universally attractive and should be the goal of *anyone* looking to improve their dating life. And this is a mistake. People aren't a monolith; we're a seething mass of individual personality types and interests. There may be overlap, but trying to apply one singular vision of what makes for a "perfect" or universally attractive lifestyle is a mistake.

And yet it's one I see all too often.

We tend to focus on a specific type of lifestyle and assume that it works for everybody. Back in my PUA days, the sum totality of my attention was focused around trying to be "the club guy" at the various hot bars downtown... and while I had a lot of success, it never really *worked* for me. I'd come home exhausted and annoyed - even when I'd gotten laid that night - because I spent the night in places where I could barely hear from the insanely loud music, reeking of cigarette smoke, paying too much for drinks and talking to people whom I barely liked. But I persisted because I thought that was "the lifestyle" for what I wanted. It wasn't until I adjusted my focus to areas that matched my personality and interests - quieter, more intimate bars, friends' parties and coffeeshops - that I realized how unsuited I was for the bar and club scene. Just as certain lifestyles tend to be incompatible with others, some lifestyles are going to be incompatible with individuals. An introvert will be uncomfortable trying to wedge themselves into being a fixture on the club-scene just as hardcore punks are going to be less likely to fit in at an exclusive country club.

You want to base your lifestyle around what works for you, not for what you think you're *supposed* to like. By following your passions, you increase the likelihood of meeting people who share your interests and values; people who, in other words, you are more likely to be compatible with. If you're into music, you're far more likely to meet someone you'll click with at a concert. If you're a high-energy person who gets a charge from large groups of people you are far more likely to meet people you'd be into at rowdy parties rather than at an open mic night or a poetry reading. If you're passionate about art, gallery shows and art history classes will be much more your speed. If you're politically active or socially minded, you will find more success volunteering your time for local politicians or non-profit organizations.

If you're not sure what it is that you're passionate about, then take some time to experiment. Give yourself permission to try things you've been curious about but never could quite bring yourself to pull the trigger on – travel, learning another language, studying a martial art, taking up a musical instrument or even something as esoteric as learning how to be a DJ. Even if it turns out not to be your thing, it can still help round you out as a person and collecting new experiences and stories is a great way to expand your personal horizons.

Finding ways to indulge and fulfill your passions and interests and making that a part of your life will naturally bring you more in contact with the sort of people you want to meet. If you're unsure about how or where to meet people who share your passions, look online. Sites like meetup.com are one of the best ways to find people who share your interests.

And don't forget to consider the type of people you want

to meet as well. To use an incredibly awkward metaphor, you need to think like a hunter stalking its prey. Successful hunters understand that they could either wander around and hope to stumble across a deer randomly, or they could stake out their watering holes and food sources... places where deer are likely to congregate. So spend some time thinking not only about the sort of things that you're interested in but the sorts of traits and values in the people you want to meet: where are they likely to hang out? What are they likely to do in their spare time, and how much crossover would there be with what you love to do?

Love Your Life

You will get the best results and the most return on your emotional investment if you love your life. The less happy you are with the direction your life is taking, the more problems you will encounter as you try to make your transformation.

Think about it: would you want to date somebody who's forever feeling miserable and worn out because they hate their job? What about somebody who was always complaining about how their hometown sucks and they'd be so much happier in another city altogether?

This is how other people will see you if you're always going on about how much your life sucks.

If you're unsatisfied with your lifestyle, it's time to sit down and examine just what it is that you feel is wrong. Do you feel stifled with where you live? Do you have a dead-end job that drains your life away and sucks out your soul? Do you not have a life outside of work or school? Do you have a strong network of friends – people who genuinely care about you as a person – or do you just have people you hang out with out of convenience but who don't share any of your interests?

This is especially true if you're having a hard time meeting the type of people you're attracted to. Sometimes the logistics work against you. You're more likely to find people interested in casual sex and one-night stands in larger metropolitan cities than you are in small, rural towns. If you're into clubs and parties, but you live out in the suburbs, you're going to have a hard time finding people in your area who hold the same interests. Some cities, by virtue of their demographics, population or even just size can be bad for dating. Many have uneven gender distribution, which can make it harder for men or women to find someone who's available. In Austin, for example, men outnumber women by 11 to 10, giving women the advantage. Manhattan, on the other hand, is better for men - there are 9.2 men for every 10 women on average. These seemingly little details can have profound effects on your dating success.

Even if it seems daunting, solving your lifestyle issues and learning how to craft a life that brings you satisfaction and fulfillment will supercharge your social life. The happier you are with who you are, the better you will be at interacting with others.

---

[1] Yes, people *do* met without leaving their home - via online dating, web forums, even through massively-multiplayer online games. That doesn't mean that you can get away with not having a life *outside* of those things.

SIX

FUN: THE MOST ATTRACTIVE PART OF A MAN

What Makes A Man Attractive

Men spend a lot of time worrying about being more attractive to women. Because of the pervasive belief that sperm is cheap and eggs are expensive – the idea that because a woman's ovum are a limited resource and biologically more difficult to produce, women grant sexual access only to those who offer the best "value" – they tend to focus on the most obvious aspects of what supposedly makes men attractive: looks and material wealth, with the nebulous idea of "status" following third.

The problem is that they're working with mistaken ideas about female sexuality; they are taking the idea that women don't like sex for sex's sake and using it to justify a profound misunderstanding of just what makes somebody appealing to women. Yeah, good looks can help – obviously, being gorgeous has an impact on one's life – but not only is it not the only thing that counts... more often than not it's not even in the top 5 of what makes a man attractive.

More than looks, more than money, more than whatever definition you want to give to "value" or "status", the most attractive aspect of a man, that x-factor that nets him attention, attraction and dates is...

...fun.

Yes. Fun. Not whether they had a perfect six-pack. Not driving an BMW or Porsche.

It was about how they made women *feel*.

Over the years as I was trying to make my transition from "The One Who Was Not Good With Girls" to "ladies man", I got to know a wide variety of folks who were good with women. Some were blessed with every advantage – classic good looks, money and charm – while others had to work for their success. And yet there were a few people in my social circle who could – to put it charitably – punch well outside of their apparent weight class. They were not classically handsome; in fact, many of them were fat, balding or both. They weren't "high-status males" with impressive jobs or flashy cars and fancy clothes. They didn't have useful contacts for the social climbers or the money for those supposed gold-diggers. They weren't secretly packing a ten-inch long cock, a prehensile tongue and the ability to breathe through their ears. They were strictly average, everyday dudes... who still managed to date sexy, intelligent, ambitious women.

Their secret was very simple: they were fun to hang around with. If you talked to them, then you were going to enjoy yourself. They knew how to make people feel good. They were authentically interesting people with stories to share and a genuine desire to get to know the people they talked to. They made friends wherever they went. The bouncers, the bartenders, the waitstaff... they all loved these guys within minutes of meeting them. Everybody knew who they were. Everybody wanted to hang out with them.

Small wonder, then, that they were so consistently successful.

The fact that they were fun to be with was all it took to flip those attraction switches. Being fun, being able to help someone enjoy themselves, transcended looks and status. It gave them a notable, long-term advantage over the guys who were all surface and flash. The ones who only had a handful of tricks and routines to rely on and the ones who got by on social pressure and status games... they might snake a girl out from under my buddies every once in a while, but they could never keep her. It didn't take very long at all before those women realized how little the flashy guys had to offer and how much my friends *really* brought to the table.

It took me a while to appreciate just what they had but once I understood, it was like a new world opened up to me. I began to see just how essential being fun was to a successful dating life... and I started to understand how to integrate it into my approach towards women.

"What Do You See In That Guy?" "He Makes Me Laugh"

It's a very simple premise: we instinctively like people who make us feel good. The better they make us feel, the more we like them. It creates a positive feedback loop: we like how they make us feel, therefore we want to spend time around them. They like us spending time with them, so they want to make us feel good.

Many of us end up wanting to spend naked time around 'em.

It's known as the Reward Theory of Attraction – we are attracted to people whose presence or behavior makes us feel appreciated and liked. When the feeling of pleasure at a person's involvement in our lives outweighs the costs - think of those someone who's funny... just so long as their making jokes about *someone else* - then we tend to be drawn towards *that* relationship over others. The brain increases dopamine and norepinephirine, which regulates the brain's pleasure and reward centers. We associate the pleasure with the person and thus want to spend more time in their presence.

This is why a sense of humor ranks so highly in every poll about what makes men attractive. It's not just a dating cliche; there are tangible, physical benefits to being with someone who can make you laugh. Laughter produces endorphins that go straight to the pleasure centers of your brain and relieves physical tension and stress in the muscles making you feel more relaxed. Making you feel good triggers the instincts that tell us that these are people we should like and enforce that feeling with a shot of dopamine.

Consider how many geeks and outcasts learned in high-school that being funny meant that the bullies and assholes would leave you alone; making people laugh helped keep you from getting your ass kicked. It was a way of not only disarming them - "hey, I'm going to make fun of myself before you have a chance to" - but it was a way of ingratiating yourself to them.

Who knew that one day you could turn it around and use those same skills as a part of a way of getting dates?

However, as much as making people feel good makes them like us, there's more to it.

Someone who is fun tends to be more confident in themselves − after all, it's hard to be fun when you're too worried about looking silly or acting childish.

For example: think of the person you know who's always the life of the party; the guy who's always the first to the dance floor, the one who's always willing to do something to get people engaged and active. He's the one who's holding court and making people laugh with his outrageous stories. He's the one who makes things fun because his sense of fun is infectious and he's not concerned with whether he's too cool or what other people will think, just so long as it makes people smile.

Or picture the quiet guy in the corner - he may not be in

the middle of things and dancing like a goofball, but he's having an intense conversation with the hottest woman in the room. Every few minutes you can hear her laugh and delivering a playful swat over something outrageous he said. He may not be the bundle of energy that the previous example is, but he's *still* making other people feel good.

So's the guy who's talking smack while playing a game of Pandemic with his date. Or the one who organized a spontaneous air-hockey tournament.

Different approaches, but same end result: They're the ones having fun, regardless of whatever's going on. They're not reliant on others to bring the good times. They have enough confidence to *make* things happen.

Fun people are also positive; excessively negative people suck the energy out of the room and kill the mood while positive people help generate energy. Fun people make others feel comfortable and have a better grasp on how to read people's signs and moods and can adjust themselves as needed.

This makes the difference between that guy I mentioned who's the life of the party, rather than someone who's just a clown: genuinely fun people can find the line and know when things are appropriate or not while a clown tends to blunder on regardless of mood or intent.

Fun As Dating Strategy

This isn't to say that it's just a matter of telling a few jokes until you manage to laugh them into bed. You want to be *fun*, not come off as though you're practicing your stand-up routine before open mic night at The Improv. Being fun is a holistic part of dating and attraction – it influences *everything* about what makes someone attractive.

Once I understood the appeal of fun, I began to

recognize how it formed the underpinnings of everything I'd learned up to that point – and how much I had seen it in action over the years.

My buddy Miles – he who attracts women the way cheese attracts mice from chapter one – was successful not *just* because he looked like the bastard son of Hugh Grant and Rob Lowe but because he was fun to be around. He was naturally outgoing and positive and instinctively understood how to make people feel good. When he focused his attention on you, you felt like the most special person in the world. He had an easy-going, good-natured charm that came from being a *genuinely* nice guy[1] who liked to tease and play around with everyone.

He didn't have a mean bone in his body; you knew, even if he was poking fun at you, that he didn't mean any harm, and he was more than willing to make fun of himself too. When he'd turn that charm and thousand-watt smile on women, they'd melt... laughing all the way back to his room.

I, on the other hand, found that banter and verbal jousting was *my* way of bringing fun to my flirting style, and the type of women *I'm* attracted to are into it as well. I have a thing for sharp, witty women who enjoy that sort of witty duel-by-wordplay; someone who can be the Myrna Loy to my William Powell, plus cocktails. When done properly, bantering is a game of verbal sparring, a back and forth interplay of wordplay, matching wits and humor with gentle ribbing and sexually charged teasing that's insanely fun for everyone involved.

Other successful ladies men I've known will use outrageous role-plays, spinning stories of how the two of them will fly off together to some tropical paradise and spend their time running a diner that specializes in American-style breakfasts for all the frustrated expats by day and camping on the beach under the stars by night.

They draw their dates in, inviting them to play along and continue the fantasy, making it even more absurd as they go until they both can't stop laughing.

One friend of mine has developed a reputation of being the **Wedding Crasher** type; whenever he's gone to a friend or family member's wedding, he inevitably hooks up with the hottest woman at the party... because he's one of the only young men who *loves* to dance. His secret is simply to be the guy everyone wants to dance with - swing, salsa, you name it, he can do it. With spins, dips and hip-swivels, he's the guy bringing women to the dance floor and escorting them back *glowing* with pleasure.

Being fun and helping others have fun is a way of keeping dates and potential relationship partners engaged and invested in you. It's a vital part of the chemistry that helps ensure that not only will she enjoy the *first* date but that she'll be interested in coming back for a *second*... and a *third*. The worst dates aren't the ones that go badly but the ones that are utterly unremarkable. A bad date can be salvaged after all; a boring date just drains the life out of everyone involved.

Building sexual tension involves understanding fun. Proper, deliberate sexual tension is like a roller-coaster ride: the deliberate slow build-up of anticipation at the very beginning cresting at the absolute height of almost unbearable frustration and the sudden thrill of the release at *just* the right moment. Even little tricks like the "almost-kiss" are built on the idea of fun; it's unselfconsciously, deliberately cheesy... and yet when delivered properly, it's silliness is a significant part of it's appeal. You're playing a naughty game like a pair of horny teenagers, seeing just how far you can push things before one or both of you simply can't stand it any longer.

Much is made about the concept of "social proof": the idea that the behavior of others is a model for how one should act. In a social context, a person with social proof –

say, a crowd of people around him has been vetted by others; people are responding positively to him, therefore he is someone others should want to get to know and pay attention to. It generates something known as the halo effect – where positive aspects of a person influence others into assuming more positive aspects about them. People like this person, therefor he must be cool.

Pick-up artists often try to manipulate social proof as a way of establishing to others that they're cool or desirable. This is often managed by trying to be surrounded by attractive women; the effect is to say "These beautiful people find me compelling; clearly they know something you don't, so *you* should find me compelling *too*."

And yet being fun is a simpler and more organic way of generating social proof – without having to rely on status games or trickery. To be fun is to bring legitimate value to an interaction rather than trying to leverage social contracts and often coercive tactics.

Think of it in terms of that guy I mentioned earlier, the one who's the life of the party. They're always the people who tend to have many people hanging around them - a desirable position to be sure.

When people see others hanging around and wanting your attention, others – like that cute brunette you've had your eyes on – will naturally gravitate towards you; they want to know what's going on that they're missing out on.

The fact that others view you as someone to spend time with will help invoke that halo effect that will make you shine even more in other's eyes.

Even if you're on the introverted side of the personality spectrum, you can make fun-as-social-proof work for you; it's a matter of establishing a reputation as much as it is about being seen in the "proper" light. Introverts often work best in one-on-one situations and so can take advantage of the situation by having interesting, intense conversations. Being fun isn't just about being the entertainer, it's about how you make others feel.

The more that you can bring a sense of fun into your dating life, the more success you will have.

How To Be Fun

The most obvious way of being fun is to be funny; after all, the appeal of a man with a sense of humor is nearly universal. However, not everybody is going to be a laugh riot, nor is it the only way to be fun.

So what are some other ways of bringing more fun into your dating life?

Pick Offbeat Dates

Everybody's done dinner and a movie; you want to stand out by taking your date somewhere different. If you can't be funny yourself, you can always borrow somebody else's sense of humor for the night and take her to a comedy club or improv performance. If you're dating a foodie, try signing up for a couple's cooking class or a wine tasting. You might go the track and watch the horse races; pick your favorites to win, even if you don't put money down on them and cheer them on. You'll be amazed at how infectious the crowd's energy can be. Find a pub that hosts a quiz-night and form your own team - pick an outrageous name for an inside joke and go head to head with other trivia buffs.

You want something different than what she's used to – novelty helps produce dopamine in the brain, after all.

Explore Your Passions

It can't be said enough: a person who explores and pursues their passions in life and can communicate them to others are people who are interesting. So many people live day-to-day humdrum lives of boring routines; having passion makes you stand out. It's an attractive trait, one that women adore because people who are passionate have drive and intensity. They have taken charge of their lives and their enthusiasm carries others along… and that is incredibly fun.

Embrace Your Competitive Side

There's nothing quite like a little rivalry to liven things up. The playful smack-talk, the tension when scores are tied, the thrill of victory… these get your hearts pumping, the juices flowing and the senses come alive. Few things are quite as fun – or arousing – as a friendly competition. Bowling, laser tag, mini-golf, go-kart racing, pool… as long as there's a contest for winner and loser, you're likely to have fun.

Master The Art of Conversation

The old adage is true: interest*ed* is interest*ing*. We love nothing more than a chance to talk about ourselves to an audience that really gets us and wants to know more. There is nothing so amazing has having an incredible, deep and in-depth discussions about life, the universe and everything… and make you both feel as though you've known each other for years instead of hours. Even if you have nothing to talk about, you can always play the Question Game. The rules are simple. First, you have to ask involved and engaging questions; no "what's your sign" bullshit. Second: you can't repeat the same question back. Third: she goes first.

Collect Stories

Just as few people have passion in their lives, few people are interested in finding new experiences. Sometimes it's worth going out and doing things just because you know there will be a story involved at the end. Take some chances and try things you've never done before… and build that bond between the two of you by experiencing them together. Whether it's exploring your city without a map or a plan and just letting whim guide you, signing up for a beginner's line-dancing session, going geocaching or even an impromptu picnic out under a blanket of shooting stars, you should make a point of finding exciting new opportunities for escapades and exploits. Sharing these new and awesome adventures will be more fun than you could ever imagine... and bring you closer together than you ever dreamed.

---

[1] But not a Nice Guy™ - someone who befriends women in hopes of collecting Nice Guy tickets that he can redeem for blow-jobs later...

Part Two:

Dating Time Wasters

SEVEN

THE APPROACH

The Least Important Part of Dating

A lot of ink has been spilled about approaching women - where to do it, how to do it, how not to do it, what you should say, how you should stand... If you go to various dating advice forums or blogs, you'll find that "I like this girl, how do I talk to her?" is possibly the most common question. Everyone knows the feeling of ball-shrinking anxiety over trying to talk to the cute brunette in our English class in high-school or approaching the girl we had a crush on at our buddy's party, or seeing that hottie at the bar with the body like wow and wishing you had the first goddamn idea of what to say to her.

And then... we don't do anything.

We sit and stew in our fear instead. We let approach anxiety take over and paralyze us. We tense up over the idea of how to talk to that attractive individual while our jerk-brains helpfully compile a long list of everything that could possibly go wrong, a Final-Destination-inspired trail of Rube-Goldberg-esque social missteps, pratfalls and screw ups that starts with saying "hello" and ends with our clawing at our freshly maced eyes while cops slam us to the floor and haul us off to a jail cell with a burly outlaw biker who is gauging our value in cigarettes.

So you might be forgiven for thinking that approaching a woman you're attracted to is one of the most important parts of dating.

And you'd be wrong.

In fact, it's possibly one of the least important parts. We only place so much emphasis on it because we've convinced ourselves that it's harder than it has to be. And that's because we tie approach anxiety in with our fears of rejection; we treat each potential approach as another opportunity for somebody to shoot us down and shred our egos. It ties into the problems with having a scarcity mentality: when you treat each and every woman you meet as being part of a rapidly dwindling pool, you're going to over-emphasize her importance to your potential dating life. A man with a scarcity mentality sees each rejection as putting him one step closer to being doomed to be single forever, eventually dying alone, unloved and forgotten.

By holding on to that sort of self-limiting belief, you're putting all of your focus on one person and letting them - a stranger, mind you - have that much control over your life. You are ceding your power to somebody you don't know and whose opinion ultimately has absolutely no relevance to your day to day existence. This is a person you may well not even have known existed yesterday... so why is she suddenly the most important person in the world?

The other fear is of being humiliated. In fact, being laughed at by women has been ranked as one of men's greatest fears in the dating world. Many of us, especially anyone who wasn't part of the "cool" crowd, can remember the fear of the mockery and insults that would come if we dared to ask out one of the popular girls back in high school. Maybe it even happened to you - you made the dubious mistake of asking out one of the school's queen-bees and found yourself the laughing stock of your grade. God knows my not-so-secret crush on the most popular girl in class back in the day made me the butt of more jokes and insults than I could count.

At the time it hurt because there was no escape from them; they were part of my day to day life and I hadn't developed the thicker skin I have today. But, over time I came to realize: I didn't really give a shit what they had to say about me. At some point I'd graduate and never have to see these people again... and that right there was the key: *I would never have to see these people again*. Who cares if they laugh? They don't exist in your life after you leave the club, the party, what-have-you.

Moreover: nobody is going to notice whether you got rejected or not. Unless you make such a huge spectacle of yourself - and by that I mean smashing objects, screaming, or otherwise acting like a crazy person - that you're drawing attention to yourself, *nobody else is paying attention to you.* They're not watching you to see if you're going to fuck up. They're far more concerned with their own issues to worry about some stranger who's not even talking to them.

In the worst case scenario... you might get shot down. But that's it. I've made more than 10,000 approaches to women and I've been shot down more often than I can easily count... and the worst I've ever had to deal with is an "ew, no".

Yes, it can be profoundly intimidating. Let's be fair: you're coming up to a total stranger and trying to get her interested in exploring the possibilities of a sexual or romantic relationship with you. This can be difficult and stressful. In a lot of ways you're making yourself emotionally vulnerable and being rejected can sometimes feel like a rejection of everything about you.

But it's only as difficult as you make it.

The Purpose of The Approach

Part of what gets people get hung up on the idea that the approach is important is that they assume that the approach will ultimately color every interaction that comes later. They worry about coming off as too needy - and thus low-status - or differentiating themselves from every other guy out there.

99% of the problems that guys have with making the approach come from trying to psych themselves up enough to actually do it. They worry about coming off as a creep, or convince themselves that they need a reason to talk to the individual - a reason, that is, other than "she's attractive". They waste energy convincing themselves that she has a boyfriend, a girlfriend or any other worst-case scenario. They spend so much time worried about whether to be direct in their approach or indirect that by the time they've actually worked up the nerve, they've exhausted themselves emotionally and end up deciding that it's just not worth it in the first place.

That ascribes far too much power to approaching someone. By approaching someone, you're trying to accomplish one thing and one thing only:

You're trying to start a conversation with them.

That's it. Everything else is window dressing. Your clever opening line? It's a detail. You are, for all intents and purposes, just stalling for time in order to hook them with your charm and and ability to hold an interesting conversation.

It's a matter of suiting your approach to your personality. If you're especially anxious about approaching a stranger, then using an indirect approach - using a question like "Can you settle a debate for us? Which 80s band sang Bizarre Love Triangle?" as a pretext to talk to someone - can make it easier to go up to somebody. If you're bolder, you can always use the direct approach of "Hi, you seem like you're cool and I wanted to meet you. My name is..." If you have a more outgoing or daring personality, you might say "I had to come talk to you or else I was going to be kicking myself for the rest of the evening."

As long as you don't start off with something along the lines of "Your skin looks soft and supple. It would make a great leather jacket", you're fine. I have started conversations (that eventually lead to either dates or sex) with "What are you drawing?", "You're very tall! High-five!", "Has anyone ever told you that you look like a Bond Girl?", "I like puppies. Your turn.", "Holy God, please tell me you're talking about something interesting. My friends just keep talking about derivatives and I'm about to blow my brains out", "Do you believe that men and women can be friends and still have sex?" and "Do you know how to cook this?"

Hell, you could just say "Pirates are inherently better than ninjas" and get away with it as long as you follow it up with an actual conversation.

There's only one rule: Don't make her uncomfortable. Proper social calibration is the important factor here. You can get away with being a little offbeat and goofy at a party, where the accepted social contract encourages talking to strangers. Coming up to a woman at a grocery store and saying "You're very blonde," is going to be off-putting, no matter how classically handsome you are. However, asking her "Hey, what spices do you think would work with this?" or "Do you know anything about $FOOD_PRODUCT?" is relevant to the situation and gets the conversation started.

And don't forget: "You seem cool and I just wanted to meet you" is almost always socially relevant.

The key to not sweating the approach is to use what I call "the Three Second Rule": if you see someone you like, you have a count of three seconds before you must go up and introduce yourself. Any longer and you just have to move on to someone else.

The Three Second Rule is there to keep your brain from going into vapor-lock; if you take longer than three seconds, you've given your brain all the time it needs to game out every single reason why you shouldn't approach and every way it could possibly go wrong.

The Fear of Failure

Let's talk about failure for a moment. We overemphasize the importance of the approach because in approaching, we immediately open ourselves to the possibility of being rejected... and rejection hurts. We naturally want to avoid this, and so we will go out of our way to minimize the myriad ways we can screw up.

But that's what comes from treating any approach that doesn't go 100% perfectly as a failure.

The hard and fast truth is: you're going to get rejected. You're going to make mistakes Even Brad Pitt doesn't go 10 for 10 when approaching women. I've watched some of the greatest lady-killers of our time flub their lines, accidentally say the wrong thing, even literally trip over themselves. Hell, I've literally choked - as in, nearly asphyxiated myself - while introducing myself to an incredibly attractive woman I met at my favorite bar.

But when you can't let the fear of failure hold you back. The more you focus on the negative outcome, the more you drain your emotional momentum, which in turn means you have to spend more time and effort rebuilding it - along with collecting the tattered remains of your ego - instead of dusting yourself off and moving on to someone else. You can't let it throw you off your game. If you allow one mistake to shatter your self-esteem and send you running home crying, then you're never going to find that special someone; you need to be willing to take the hits when they come.

Not every interaction has to be perfect. As long as you don't actively offend the person you want to meet - if they're still willing to talk to you, then you're still doing just fine. You can bounce back from almost any mistake as long as you don't let it destroy you as soon as it happens. I've even stopped myself in the middle of talking to somebody when I realized that I'd just shoved my foot in my mouth and said "You know what? I really don't like where that was going. Let's try that again", walked away and then walked right back and introduced myself as though I were meeting them for the first time. The audaciousness of the move - and the fact that I wasn't going to let a simple mistake freak me out - made her laugh out loud. What could have sunk the interaction then became a key part of "the story of how we met". It was a completely unplanned, organic moment. If I'd spent any time obsessing about my approach, it would've sunk me... but by de-emphasizing it's importance and realizing that the real draw was my ability to make her laugh and generate chemistry, I was able to snatch victory from the jaws of defeat and take her home that night.

Don't sweat the approach. Spend your energy on the parts that matter - that come after you say "hello".

EIGHT

SOCIAL STATUS

The Over-Importance of Status

There's an obsession with the concept of value and status when you're dealing with men's dating advice. The idea is that, when you boil everything down, women are attracted to high-value, high-status men; therefore, men who want to be more successful with women should be as high-value as possible.

Don't get me wrong: social status and value are definitely attractive... but they're not the end-all, be-all that people seem to think they are.

Especially when we keep getting the definitions of value wrong.

The most common definitions of high-value or high-status men - much like the idea of an "attractive lifestyle - is in the measure of their material wealth. The complaint that women only want rich men is a common stereotype. It's often a tenet of evolutionary psychology that women instinctively look for the best providers; thus it gets extrapolated that women get the screaming thigh-sweats as soon as they see a man flash a Patek Philippe watch or who have a whiff of beluga caviar on them. Nobody really believes that Anna-Nicole Smith married an octogenarian billionaire because of pure animal attraction, right?

Of course, this is easily disprovable; a quick trip to your local Wal-Mart will find plenty of folks in happy relationships, despite their distinct lack of Hermes, Bugatti or Swiss bank accounts. In my own life I've known many men of privilege – ranging from "comfortably well-to-do" to "richer than God" – who had the same troubles with women that I did. Money by itself clearly didn't buy love for them; it didn't even give them that much of an advantage at the negotiating table.

Money is good at attracting women... who only want money, and aren't too concerned about who provides it.

What about power? Noted playboy and war criminal Henry Kissinger once quipped that "Power is the ultimate aphrodisiac", and Lord knows that the man got more ass than a drunk at a donkey auction with a stolen credit card, despite the fact that he looks like the Goblin King. And I don't mean the one with the muppets and the codpiece.

To be fair, some people *are* attracted to power. But at the same time, Kissinger was also a political animal who thrived i n a w o r l d o f i n f l u e n c e - p e d d l i n g and Machiavellian manipulation; this is not an arena where the socially awkward get ahead. It's the job of the Secretary of State to be able to charm and influence others. And after all, a man who was able to negotiate détente with Russia wasn't going to be flummoxed by a pretty lady.

What about fame? It certainly helps – Kevin Bacon once mentioned that "any idiot can get laid if they were famous". But it's clearly not the end-all, be-all – after all, Ray-J isn't exactly the last of the Red Hot Lovers despite having been propelled to momentary stardom by association with Kim Kardashian. Does a socially desirable job make one higher status? I've known plenty of lawyers, doctors, actors, musicians and DJs who have all had miserable dating lives.

You see, the second mistake is to assume that value and status are universal – that certain things are always going to be respected more highly across the board, regardless of when and where they occur.

Humans as a whole aren't a hive-mind. We're part of diverse and varied communities, and what marks you as high status in one is going to mean jack in another. Not everybody is going to be impressed by the same things; a venture capitalist may be used to being king of all he surveys in the corporate world, but nobody's going to give a shit about him at a comic convention. I've had pleasant conversations with actors, rockers and porn stars and kept my cool, but I absolutely lost my goddamn monkey mind the first time I had a chance to talk to Peter S. Beagle. Penn Jillette has stated more than once that he'd rather party with rocket scientists than rock stars. Robert Kirkman and Brian K. Vaughn are beloved comic writers and respected names in television and film, with multiple Eisner awards to their names, but if you drop them in the middle of a NBA playoffs, more people are going to flip their shit when they see Tim Duncan or Manu Ginobli walking by. The scene girl isn't going to flock to a lawyer in an Armani suit, not when Jimmy Urine from Mindless Self Indulgence is around. The women at a nightclub are going to be far more interested in the club promoters or the DJ or the guys who can get them into the VIP section than Patrick Rothfuss, while Neil Gaiman's female fans are less likely to squee over Kobe Bryant.

So yes, the jocks in high school do have value... within the context of high-school. And even then, it's only in people who value high-school sports. So in West Texas, the football player may be a god among men, but if you drop him in the middle of Manhattan... well, he's just another guy.

You Can't Fake Value

One of the common complaints I heard in my time on the Austin dating scene was that every guy was telling women that either he was a photographer (the better to invite them back to his studio for - ahem - art photos) or in a band. In Dallas, every guy claimed to be a DJ and in Houston, everyone was in the oil business. In New York, every guy's a Wall Street hustler, in DC they're a consultant, and in LA everyone's an actor, a writer or a producer.

It's not uncommon for guys to try to enhance their resume a little in the name of impressing women; they drop an extra hundred for the Hermés belt (with the big H buckle of course- what good is it if women don't know it's Hermés?) to look richer or promote themselves from a drone in Accounts-Receivable to a major player in Acquisitions. They'll puff up their vacations from a weekend in Corpus Christi to a week in South Beach, name drop when they think they can get away with it and basically lie through their teeth in order to appear cooler than they are.

A lot of classic pick-up artist techniques are all about faking status and conveying that you're actually high-value through behavior and appearing to be less-invested in the interaction... all while desperately wanting to get into her pants. Negging, for example, is intended to convey to a beautiful woman (who is – by PUA definitions – a high-status target) that you have higher social status than she does by being willing to covertly insult her; after all, most guys are going to be so intimidated by her beauty that they'd never dream of giving a left-handed compliment like "nice nails... are they real?" By conveying your higher status – and bringing her down a peg – the woman is then theoretically supposed to become more attracted and actively seek your approval.

Similarly, many of the canned routines from PUA culture – especially classics like the C's vs. U's or Crazy Stripper Ex – are intended to subtly convey higher status by implying that you've dated an elite class of women before, usually models or actresses. These pre-packaged conversations are designed to make the individual using them seem more interesting and important while helping them convey sexual interest without seeming too interested; after all, being too invested in getting her home is a sign of low status and, thus, unattractive.

The problem is that you can't fake value. You can baffle people with your bullshit for only so long before they start to notice. Even the best poker players have their tells and the truth inevitably wins out. It's easy to pretend that you're unaffected by someone's beauty, but unless you are genuinely unaffected by them, they're going to start picking up on all the subtle behavioral tics you're giving off. You may be talking about your model ex-girlfriend but women will start noticing that you can't look them in the eye for very long, that your body language starts to change as soon as you're distracted, and that you're more nervous around them than someone of your supposed status would be.

Moreover, women are used to guys lying about themselves – ask any woman about men lying about their height or physique in online dating sites. Just about every woman who has spent any time in the dating scene - or hell, who went through high-school - is going to be familiar with the ways that guys will embellish themselves in order to look better; after all that time, they are quite good at spotting incongruities.

Value is inherent; if you don't have it, you're going to give yourself away in hundreds of little tells and no amount of verbal trickery or manufactured gloss is going to make up for that lack.

What IS Value, Then?

So after all of that talk about what status isn't, let's talk about what it is.

Put simply: value and status are about what you bring to

the table as a person. Money can help; people do value wealth after all. But having money in and of itself isn't status or value; money can do many things but it can't buy you charm or class, and the people who are attracted to it tend to only be interested in the money. The same goes for power – power without actual value attracts users and manipulators who want to use that power for themselves - or to take it if they can. Fame brings people looking for a little reflected glory – look at all of the would-be starlets of both genders who've tried to make a name for themselves by talking about how they fucked Kanye or Kim Kardashian or (shudder) Pauly D. Geraldine Edwards, one of the original groupies and the inspiration for Penny Lane in **Almost Famous,** wanted to be considered a muse; she wasn't sleeping with musicians because of their charming personalities, but because she wanted to be a part of the creative process.

Real status and value come from how you act and how you make others feel. If you have an attractive lifestyle, if you know how to connect with people and to make them feel good, *then* you have value.

Can you inspire respect in other people, not through your material goods or being famous but through what you have to offer as a person? That's status. Can you bond with people on an emotional level and make them feel as though you understand them better than anyone else does? Then you have higher social value than someone who is only able to meet someone on the surface, who is all glitz with no substance to back it up.

Someone with an abundance mentality - a man who understands that there are millions of women in the world and that rejection isn't any big deal. This man is going to display higher value than someone with a scarcity mentality - someone who treats every conversation with a woman as the last chance he's ever going to have for love or sex. Someone with strong boundaries is higher-status than someone who lets others walk all over him – after all, if he can't respect himself, why should anyone else? Someone who is secure enough in himself to be his authentic self – unafraid to embrace his flaws and who doesn't feel the need to impress others – is higher-status than the man who is obsessed with what others think of him. Someone who is at ease with himself and others is going to be higher status than someone who is constantly focused on being the alpha male of the group, trying to dominate every conversation and interaction to ensure his place in the hierarchy.

This is why the unemployed musician - the one with ambition and motivation, who's scrambling for every gig he can get and constantly pushing the limits of his talent – is more appealing to women than the shallow stockbroker with the Audi coupe who's sucking up to his bosses as he tries to climb the corporate ladder. That musician brings more to everyone he meets; his confidence, his drive and willingness to persevere are of higher value than the ability to kiss ass and fellate egos. This is why a life-long millionaire can be as awkward as a pauper, even as he insists he's better than the hoi polloi.

Focusing on status and social proof only means that you don't have it. Live your life, authentically and courageously and value will come to you without having to think about it.

NINE

REJECTION

The Only Thing We Have To Fear...

We all worry about rejection. Everyone, from the virgin who's never even been kissed to the most experienced pick-up artist fears being rejected. We're all familiar with that pain; it leaves you feeling like you're the lowest of the low, like someone just kicked your soul in the nuts. It's like your very existence is being judged and found wanting. Being rejected can feel as though it's a response to you as a person rather than a reaction to the circumstance or situation. You feel humiliated. You feel like not only did everybody just watch you get shot down, but they're all enjoying watching you being put back in your place. Now news of your failure is spreading like wildfire through your entire community, leaving you emotionally isolated as an object of ridicule who will never, ever have sex again, even with yourself.

Whether it's summoning up the courage to go flirt with the cute girl at the party or finally mustering up the nerve to ask out the co-worker that you've been interested in for the longest time, the fear of being rejected that keeps most people from even so much as making the first step, never mind actually getting as far as asking somebody out on a date.

Notice very carefully that I said it's the fear of getting rejected that holds people back. Much like many other phobias, it's the anticipation of rejection – more than the rejection itself – that causes people to hesitate. We're not avoiding rejection itself so much as the physical symptoms that we feel at the idea of being rejected.

We are, quite frankly, afraid of being afraid. And we do it to ourselves.

One perk of the human experience is the power of our imagination - because we can embrace abstract reasoning and comprehend the passage of time, we're capable of creating entire experiences that exist solely in our minds… ones that our brains accept as real. Studies using fMRIs have found that the act of imagining something and accessing a memory of something sends blood to the same portion of the brain. Moreover, studies have found that visualization of practicing a task is almost equal to actually doing it.

But as awesome as this is, it also has a drawback: because our brains accept imaginary experiences as genuine stimulus, what we imagine going badly affects us just as much as it would if it actually happened. So whenever we start to imagine all the ways that it's going to hurt when we get rejected, we actually feel them. And because we instinctively avoid things that hurt us, we get wrapped up in fears based on the anticipation of what's about to happen. So not only are we imagining all the horrible things that could happen when we make ourselves vulnerable to someone we're attracted to, but we're experiencing all of the physical symptoms of fear on top of it - elevated heart-rate, the way our throats seem to close up, the uncontrollable shivers as our brain dumps adrenaline into our system. Our bodies react as though it is *literally* a life and death situation… and so our brains make the association between the potential of rejection and the possibility of dying.

As a result, the expectation of being rejected is so

disturbing that many people will do almost anything to avoid it. But rather than trying to minimize the fear, they end up trying to immunize themselves against everything they imagine will happen to them when (not if) they get shot down... and that almost always means not taking the chance in the first place.

Oh, they'll have very good reasons why they couldn't possibly go up to that person, or ask her out on a date. You don't know if she's single. Or she's with her friends and you'd rather wait until she's alone. Or you're just not feeling social right now. Or you want to wait until you've done something that makes you feel worthy of asking her out. They're all very good, very plausible reasons... but the end result is always the same: they excuse us from having to face the fear of rejection.

However, trying to avoid rejection is a waste of time and energy.

You Can't Control How People React

The problem with spending time worrying about or trying to avoid rejection is that you simply cannot ever control how people will respond to you. It's something I've encountered a lot in my time as an advice columnist and dating coach - guys who say "I like this girl, I asked her out and she shot me down. How can I get her to go out with me?" Another common variation is "How do I get girls to stop flaking out on me before dates?"

And the unfortunate truth is: you can't. More often than not, the answer is "It was never going to happen in the first place, and you should really just let her go." But that's usually not the answer that people want to hear; they want to hear "Ok, this is the magic formula to never having to worry about getting shot down ever again. Here's how you get her so unbelievably horny for you that she'll never even *dream* of flaking on you."

But if that's what you're looking for, you may as well quit talking to me - or any dating coach, for that matter - and find yourself a New Age shop and invest in crystals and love potions instead, because you're asking for hoodoo, not actual advice. You're looking for mind control powers and those simply don't exist.

Actually, I take that back. You should just give that money to me directly. It'll do you just about as much good, but at least you'll be contributing to a worthy cause: keeping me in groceries.

Take flaking, for example. Having a woman you're interested suddenly cancel a date - or worse, just not show up - blows goats; in many ways, it's the emotional equivalent of Lucy yanking the football away from Charlie Brown. So, naturally, guys who've had girls flake on them want to know how to make them stop. And where there's a need, people will rush to fill it. There are any number of blogs and websites out there that will quite cheerfully sell you their "patented anti-flake technique", guaranteed to ensure that any woman you ask out will never cancel on you at the last minute. They may advise you to play various head-games, to flake first or even to call her out on it... but none of that is going to actually make her show up, because at the end of the day, if she's flaking on you, it's because *she just wasn't that into you in the first place.*

You're trying to make her like you. And you can't. The only answer is to do a better job building chemistry and sexual attraction with the next woman you meet.

It may be that you deserve to get rejected. You may have poor social calibration and so creeped her out by accident, without noticing you did. You may not have built up any sexual chemistry and she just sees you as a platonic friend. You may have said something offensive, pissed her off, or pushed too hard.

But sometimes you can do everything right and still get

rejected simply because of some x-factor that you couldn't possibly account for. In fact, you'll frequently get rejected for reasons that have absolutely nothing to do with you. You may look like her asshole ex who stole her money and fucked her best friend. She may have had a fight with her Mom and is only at the bar because she's trying to get a beer in her before she decides to choke a bitch. She may have just gotten out of a tumultuous relationship and isn't ready to date anyone right now. Or you may simply be the fifth, or sixth or twentieth guy to hit on her that night and she's PMS'ing so her emotions are all out of whack and she's behind on her credit card payments and she *just can't fucking deal with any of this right now, ok?*

Why would you let this affect your self-esteem? You can't control her emotions, you can't make her like you... so why are you getting torn up over it?

It's Never As Bad As You Think

Cold hard truth time: you're going to get rejected. It's just how the world works. Even if you're Studly Goodnight with George Clooney's swagger, Ron Jeremy's cock and Bill Gates' paycheck, there will be women out there who simply just won't be interested in you for any number of reasons. Show me someone who has never been rejected and I'll show you someone who's never taken a chance, ever.

Not trying, in many ways, is actually more comfortable; when you don't actually make the attempt, then you can live in perpetual hope of what might happen, without actually taking any risk of getting your dreams shattered. You can enjoy the mental glow of the potential success instead of putting your ego on the line in reality and having to face the potential of rejection. No matter how bad things get - whether you're watching other happy couples with poisonous envy or lamenting your dateless life - you can hold on to the hope of the potential relationship to pull you through.

Ironically enough, that potential actually makes it worse. Ask any artist or writer: there's nothing quite so intimidating as a blank page or canvas, full of infinite possibilities. The greater the potential for success, the greater the chances for catastrophic failure.

Unfortunately, potential without the will behind it is wasted. Spending time focused on what you could do is nothing but mental masturbation; it might feel good but it's getting you nowhere. All you are doing is expending mental energy on a poor substitute for actual success that will ultimately leave you unfulfilled and dissatisfied... and more importantly, teaches you nothing.

So if you're going to try to date at all, you're going to get rejected. And let's be fair: rejection, whether it's by a relative stranger or by someone you have known and longed for for ages, sucks. However, it's also not the end of the world scenario that you've conjured up in your head.

All of these scenarios are built up on the expectation of embarrassment and judgement. You're afraid of being humiliated in front of others, whether it's by your boss after you just asked for a raise or by that hot librarian working the reference desk after you asked her for her number. You can just picture her breaking out into a harsh laugh, hardly believing that you had the gall to ask her for her number, calling her friends over to witness your shame. You can hear how everybody hoots and laughs at you while you slink away with your tail between your legs, wishing you could just jump into a crevasse and pull it in after you.

In reality though? That's not going to happen.

When you've made your move and been rejected... all that's happened is that you've been turned down. That's it. Yeah, it blows that you didn't get what you wanted, but as far as such things go, not getting a number or a date or what-have-you is pretty minor in the scheme of things.

Everything else? That's entirely in your head. Nobody's pointing and laughing. Nobody else is going to notice – or even care. Hell, anyone who does happen to see it won't even remember five minutes later. It's not an indictment of you as a person. It's just a simple "no, thank you".

Once you learn to accept this, you'll be able to make the steps towards turning rejection from an earth-shattering event to "no big deal". Of course, the best way to do this is... well, through experience. That is, to be rejected a few times. And that's the tough part.

But in the end, it's not about you. Like I said earlier: the first thousand rejections don't count, any more than the strikes count when you're first learning how to play baseball, or the grammatical mistakes count when you're learning a new language. You're still in the process of learning. And part of that learning process means getting used to the idea that sometimes people aren't going to want to date you and that's just *fine*.

Rejection Means You Were Incompatible

A lot of people take rejection as an indictment of their worth as an individual; that if they were a better person on the whole, they wouldn't have been shot down. They take being unable to get a woman's phone number, or to get her to call them back, or that first date, or a second date, or sex as proof that they are somehow deficient or sub-par in comparison to a world where everybody else seems to succeed with so much ease.

This is an excellent example of a self-limiting belief - by attributing your failure to some unseen imperfection or fault, you actually rob yourself of the ability to get better. Failure is merely not getting the desired result - in this case, a date, a number, a handie in the bathroom, what have you. When you equate the idea of rejection with failure and make it into some horrific state to be avoided at all costs, you make it impossible to look at it dispassionately and objectively and to learn from it.

And one of the most important things you can learn is that rejection often means that you were fundamentally incompatible in the first place.

Rejection, quite frankly, can be a good thing. If you're being genuine, your true self as opposed to trying to be what you think people should like, then a woman rejecting you is doing you a favor. You're finding out that there's a reason why the two of you would never work. You may not have been their type, which means you wouldn't have worked out in the long run. You may have a physical feature they find unattractive, which is fine because you want someone who's into you. If you're into science fiction or video games or comics and she doesn't like geeks, then you're better off being rejected; after all, you wouldn't want to date someone who doesn't respect your passion and interests.

Unfortunately, our egos often get caught up in our dating lives and when this happens, we tend to take rejection personally. Especially when we're rejected by someone whom we think is just being a bitch. It's tempting to want to want to take her down a peg. To break down her defenses and make her realize that no, you really are attractive and she should give you a chance. Oh to be sure, you can spend a lot of your precious time and energy to try to change "disinterested" to "interested"[1], but it's still not going to change the fact that she's an asshole. By rejecting you, she's let you know early on that you're better off finding somebody else who digs what you have to offer.

Rejection hurts, but trying to avoid it is impossible and a waste of time. You can devote all that effort to trying to prevent it or to winning over someone you don't really like in the first place... or you can shrug your shoulders, never give her another thought and find someone who actually wants to talk to you.

---

[1] SPOILER ALERT: You won't.

Part Three:

Where Dating Goes Wrong

TEN

SHORT CUTS AND MAGIC BULLETS

You Can't Short-Cut The Dating Process

Nobody understands the frustrations that come with dating better than I do.

You already feel as though you're missing out on something that everybody else just gets instinctively. You look back on all of your dating mishaps and misfires and missed opportunities and want nothing more than to start making up for all of that lost time right now. Being told that getting better at dating takes time and practice doesn't help; you're Luke Skywalker chomping at the bit to be a Jedi while Yoda's telling you that you need to learn patience. You want the sex life of your dreams bad and you want it now.

And there are plenty of people out there who are willing to sell you those short-cuts. The problem is what they're selling: snake-oil. Bullshit and placebos dressed up as advice and packaged to convince you that it's the guaranteed cure for all of your dating issues.

This is one of the biggest issues I have with the self-help movement in general and the Pick-Up Artist community in particular: the idea that there is some magic bullet, some special trick or formula that will let you leapfrog over all of the real work and drop you straight into the Player's Life that you've always wanted. The problem with this is that most problems with dating come either from ignorance or personal issues and there simply isn't any substitute for actual hard-won experience. Most of the time, these short-cuts offer ways of trying to plaster over any underlying issues and substitute trickery for personal growth; other times they're simply the verbal or intellectual equivalent of paying for Dumbo's magic feather - essentially just another way to psych yourself up and bolster your confidence rather than anything that actually teaches you how to do better in the long run.

Now, I'm all in favor of somebody making a buck - after all, you've presumably paid for the book you're reading - but trying to rely on these short-cuts ultimately retards your actual growth; in fact, in many cases it will actively make you worse.

There are two ways of getting better at dating. In one, you learn how to be manipulative and use social arm-twisting and techniques derived from high-pressure sales tactics in order to coerce vulnerable people into doing what you want. In the other, you learn to be a more interesting person. And having done both... the former has a very limited shelf-life. After all, you simply can't fake an amazing lifestyle or being an interesting person; no matter how good an actor you think you are, you will almost inevitably be caught out because women simply aren't stupid. Moreover, it rots your soul; when your social life is a competition of trying to enforce your will on others, you *will* hit the wall. Almost every person I've known who has tried to use these short-cuts - myself included - has had their long dark night of the soul where they inevitably realize how little they actually have.

You need to be a genuine person in order to get better at dating, and you will never get there if you rely on these placebos.

So let's look at a couple of the more common ones that you're likely to run into.

Canned Routines

One of the highlights of the PUA community is the use of canned material – pre-scripted opening lines like the famous "jealous girlfriend", pseudo-cold reads like "C's vs. U's" or "The Cube", stories and routines sourced from other people via message boards, forums, sub-reddits, ebooks and blogs. These are designed to create the illusion of social experience and emotional fluency while simultaneously giving women the impression that you are a "high-status male", thus convincing them to find you far more fuckable than if you were to just approach them like a normal person.

Canned material has been part of the PUA handbook almost from its inception, whether it was via hypnotic conversational patterns, neuro-linguistic programming anchors and Speed Seduction to just sharing material that may or may not have worked via online communities. These routines supposedly convey attractive attributes like hinting that you're used to dating beautiful women, that you have a desirable job or lifestyle or just that you lead a life of adventure and excitement.

In short, you're borrowing somebody else's lifestyle to substitute for your own; it's the verbal equivalent of trying to convince people that you own the beach-front mansion that belongs to a friend of yours, or hoping that nobody notices your BMW is a rental.

Even as the trends in the community moved to "natural" game (that is, trying to make it look like you're not running pick-up material), routines have been part of the backbone of the industry.

Now while there is value to be found in eliminating the

"I don't know what to say!" panic moments that may cause your brain to vapor-lock and leave you stammering like an idiot, canned routines are effectively training-wheels for being able to carry on a conversation like a normal person. The use of routine stacks – layers of routines used in a particular order so as to invoke specific emotional effects – becomes a substitute for having an actual personality and experiences of your own. It ends up being an attempt to treat picking women up as though you were facing down a raid boss in World of Warcraft; follow this specific plan of attack and it'll all work out the way you want. You want to lower her defenses, so you start off with the Jealous Girlfriend opener, then the Best Friends Test to disarm her friend followed by Crazy Stripper Ex to raise buying temperature and then go in for the kill by using Rings On Fingers and Strawberry Fields to convince her she's actually a very sexual person...

It's dating via flow-chart: IF a THEN SAY b ELSE SAY c, THEN RUN SUB-ROUTINE x.

The problem, of course, is that eventually the material is going to run out. At some point you're going to hit the end of the routine and then you're left with whatever you bring to the table on your own... and that's when the cracks in your made-up identity start to show. You've been trying to borrow somebody else's words in order to give your own a little spit and polish, but eventually you're going to have to be yourself – and if you've banked your entire persona on your routines, then any attraction you've managed to build is going to come crashing down around your ears.

Using canned material also puts all of the focus on the wrong place. The idea that you can seduce a woman by using specific stories to flip her attraction switches is a nice idea, but it has less to do with the words and much more with the person. I've never had a woman suddenly decide she wanted to go to bed with me because I told her she had a c-shaped smile unlike my implied model ex-girlfriend's ushaped smile; it was more about creating an emotional connection, not my supposed demonstrations of value. Did I make her laugh and feel good? Did I present myself well? Did I know how to generate that all-important "spark"?

Now I do recommend having a couple of good jokes on reserve that you can pull out as needed, or having a few good stories up your sleeve. That being said, there's a difference an oft-told story about your trip to Cambodia when you climbed to the top of Ankor Thom to watch the sun set and met a hot Scottish backpacker only to have her carried away by her man-mountain boyfriend[1] and relying on a pre-scripted crutch to get you through an interaction, which is going to come off as canned and awkward.

"Just Be Alpha, Bro"

If there is one recurring magic bullet that drives me crazy, it's the idea of evolutionary psychology; specifically, that women are attracted to the "alpha" male. The idea is simple: there are alphas and there are betas. Alphas are the leaders of the pack; the betas are the followers. The alphas get the best of everything – the best food, the most resources and the lion's share of the women. The betas get the scraps... if they're even that lucky. Women, of course, are programmed via evolution to only want alpha males; they may shack up with the beta for material support and child-rearing, but they'll sneak off behind the beta's back to go bang the alphas.

It's an idea with appeal: it is easy to apply in the macro view – submissive, needy men aren't terribly appealing to the majority of women after all – and offers a one-size-fits-all solution to sex and dating. Want more women? Just be more "alpha" and they'll come flocking to your door like mice to peanut butter.

It's also based on a complete misunderstanding of both

evolution and psychology and attempts to translate (mistaken) social hierarchical models from chimpanzees to humans.

The first and obvious problem is that humans aren't chimpanzees. We're far closer, genetically, to bonobos. Chimps don't mate outside of estrus; bonobos and humans do. Human and bonobo males have larger testicles than chimpanzees do, while human and bonobo females have vulva that are oriented towards the front; chimpanzee females have rear-oriented vulva. Humans and bonobos have oxytocin receptors in the brain - that is, we have parts of the brain that are designed specifically to respond to the chemicals that encourage feelings of social bonding and closeness that are produced at orgasm. Chimpanzees don't.

The second problem is the way it promotes a disturbing attitude towards women; the cult of the "Alpha Male" believes that all women are, in effect, whores who will cheerfully ditch a guy as soon as a better offer comes along. All women. This includes your mother, your sisters, your aunts, your cousins and that hot redhead you've had a crush on since forever. Coming into any interaction with women with the belief that they're just looking for Mr. GoodBar and will trade up at the earliest opportunity is going to ensure that you're never going to have the success you're hoping for.

The next problem is that the idea of what's "alpha" is a subject up for much debate. The definition of what is alpha becomes a weird Rorschach test, exposing what the individual believes defines "masculinity" combined with a "don't give a fuck" attitude. Is a banker more "alpha" than a musician? What if the banker loses his job? Is the outlaw biker more "alpha" than the club promoter? Is it more alpha to fuck as many women as possible or to be able to commit to a single woman and raise a family? Most forms of recommended "alpha" behavior waver between "cocky/ funny" responses to basic questions, ignoring what women are saying and being as socially domineering as possible. The obsession with alpha behavior carries over into mixed groups or even all-male groups; there can be only one alpha after all, and even friendly hang-outs can turn into constant competitions for status as people try to assume the socially dominant position. Does an "alpha" male buy drinks for girls he meets at bars? Does he change his plans in order to make allowances for others? Does he befriend the other guys in the group, or does he try to stare them down and otherwise intimidate them into leaving?

If you're the sort of person who feels as though they've always been powerless or weak, whose girlfriend cheated on them with some douchebag... this idea can be appealing. It's a variation of the Will to Power; become an alpha male and revel in the power and status that has been so long denied to you. Learn how to assert yourself and watch the world become your oyster. Men will fear you, women will supplicate and life will be nothing but a rap video for you from now until the heat death of the universe.

Of course the problem is that *it's not real*. The idea of being "alpha" is appealing in its simplicity - a dating philosophy you can fit on a bumper sticker – but humans and human sexuality are anything but simple. By trying to reduce everything to a binary state – alpha and beta, leaders and followers – and applying that philosophy to everything, all that happens is you end up with a bunch of men trying to overcompensate for their own perceived weaknesses by acting like overly-macho, selfish, chauvinistic idiots.

Human relationships are insanely complicated and defy easy explanations. Even amongst apes, the "alpha" status doesn't mean what people like to pretend that it does. Alpha males don't get the majority of sex because the females are instinctively attracted to them; they get it by beating the shit out of other males, if the alpha doesn't *straight-up murder them*. And even then, the threat of violence doesn't keep the betas from getting laid; the betas are frigging in the rigging as soon as the alpha's back is turned.

Confidence and assertiveness is indeed sexy, while neediness is the Anti-Sex Equation, but trying to be "alpha" is just a way of trying to shortcut growing one's self-esteem by acting like a cock.

Status Games

Speaking of overcompensating: we've talked before about the mistake of obsessing over one's status and value. There have been studies (amongst college students, with the inherent problems that comes with relying exclusively on them as test-subjects) that status can be an influence in attraction. The problem, however, is just how one *conveys* that value.

This is where the idea of value-as-short-cut comes in.

Part of the idea of running "game" on people is that it's a way of trying to make yourself look higher status than you really are – at least in the short term. Establish your value as higher than others' – especially your target - and it's blowjobs and champagne all around.

There is no better illustration of this idea than the "neg", for example – one of the longest running memes in pick-up, and the one I wish I could single-handedly eliminate from the dating lexicon. The "neg" – as developed by Mystery – is a strategic insult or left-handed compliment. Depending on who you talk to, a "neg" is intended either to reduce the other person's self-esteem (and therefore her social value) and make her crave validation from you or to establish that you are so unfazed by her beauty or social status that you're willing to give her shit, thus implying that you are at an equal or higher status. Either way, you are essentially trying the age-old technique of pulling the pig-tails of the girl you like.

The idea of "cocky-funny" is also a way of establishing one's supposed status in the social hierarchy: by going beyond "confidence" and well into "I'm the greatest thing since World War III" mode, telling vaguely insulting jokes at somebody else's expense is supposed to be a way of saying "Hey, I must be high status because why else would I be willing to make fun of a hot girl?"

In reality, most of what it says is "Hi, I'm a raging asshole who thinks it's funny to be rude to people in hopes of bending them to my will."

Similar status games are often tied in with the use of canned routines mentioned earlier – certain routines are popular because they contain inherent "demonstrations of higher value", such as implying that you have ex-girlfriends who are models or strippers, a high-status job or financial success. Getting bottle-service at a club is another way of trying to prove status – you're in the VIP section after all.

Other ways of trying to fake one's status involve applying mind games and low-level abuser tactics and trying to "flip the script" on women. For example, if a woman won't respond to texts or phone-calls, the would-be player will "punish" the woman by putting them on "text probation" or using communication freeze-outs in hopes of making the supposedly-misbehaving person try to win back the player's approval.

All of these little tricks are designed with one goal in mind: to successfully entice someone who is otherwise "out of your league" into sleeping with you. But as with canned material, you quickly fall upon a singular problem: it's all based on bullshit. Women aren't stupid, and they're very used to men trying to artificially inflate their dating resumes. Any woman who's spent any time on the dating scene knows to look for tricks like these. It doesn't take very much to make other people realize that the person they're talking to is full of shit, and any attraction that they might have built up is lost like tears in an over-used Blade Runner reference.

Using status games betrays a very simple issue: the desperate need to impress the other person and win their approval by trying to convince them to seek yours. People who are legitimately awesome don't have to spend their time telling other people how awesome they are. The attempt to game one's supposed status is one of the surer signs of being low status. Trying to fake your way into dating "out of your league" only establishes one thing: that the other person is indeed out of your league, because you don't bring enough to the table.

Building emotional connections is more reliable way of building attraction (and status) than trying to artificially inflate yourself – or to drag someone down to your level instead. A broke musician who can make a woman feel like the most special person in the world is going to be far more attractive than the guy in the shiny suit who's busy trying to convince others that he's a music mogul and running compliance checks on a woman to make sure she's buying his crap.

There's No Substitute for Practice

The cold hard truth is that tricks, gimmicks and games are no substitute for genuine connection. And the only way you're going to learn how to do this is to go out and practice.

It can seem counter-intuitive to try to practice human interactions - after all, you're trying to do something that other people seem to know how to do instinctively. But dealing with other people is a skill, and one that you can only improve via actually using it. And this means going out and simply flirting with people.

This can be difficult if you are hung up on the idea that

you need to be liked by every woman you talk to. You have to be willing to accept that you're going to fuck up, offend people and get rejected. If you keep a scarcity mentality and believe that every rejection is just one step closer to being forever alone, you will never be able to actually improve; you will be too invested in an ideal outcome to actually take risks and make mistakes.

Just as sports teams will have scrimmages to brush up their readiness, you want to interact with people when you have no investment in the outcome other than getting better. This may mean just going out and approaching as many people as possible. It may mean going to a strip club and flirting with the dancers, understanding that they're not going to date you or go home with you. It may mean being willing to go on dates just for the sake of going on a date with someone rather than as a prelude to sex or romance.

But regardless of how you practice, you need to put in the time. It is literally the only way to get better.

You can find some limited success in using "game" to gloss over your issues, but not only will it not last for very long but it will leave you in a worse state than you were in before; people can spot a faker and the trade off is never worth it. To improve your game, you need to improve yourself. You don't need canned openers or scripted material, you just need to know how to talk to people. You need assertiveness, not poorly understood ideas of what masculinity means. You need to lead a life that's vibrant and full, to know your worth and to act on that, rather than trying to prove yourself or attempting to impress others with a false front.

Don't look for the one secret, the short-cut, the magic bullet that will solve all your ills.

They don't exist.

The only answer is to do the work.

---

[1] True story, by the way.

ELEVEN

THE PERIL OF THE FIRST DATE

A Great First Date is NOT an Interview

Believe it or not, the first area where guys screw up the most isn't getting the date, but in the first date itself.

First dates can be stressful. You're trying to find the right balance of "impressive" but "nonchalant". You're stressing over where to take her, what to say, who's going to pay for what and – most of all – do you go for the kiss at the end of the night? Then, of course, if everything goes well, is there going to be a second date or are you going to be waiting by the phone that never rings, desperately trying to summon up your latent telepathy so you can implant the idea of calling you back via thought projection?

The problem is that so many people fall back on two of the oldest, hoariest cliches: the coffeehouse date and the ever classic "dinner and a movie".

A great first date really isn't that complicated. You want to focus on three things: fun, conversation and a hint of sexual tension. You want your date to go home thinking about what a great guy she just hung out with and how much fun it would be to see him again. You don't want a date to be an awkward interview session, where you sit across from one another and grill each other with the ten standard getting-to-know-you questions over cups of rapidly cooling coffee before awkwardly protesting that no, you are going to pay for the drinks.

This is one of the reasons I prefer to avoid the coffee date and the dinner-and-a-movie date: they're cliche and boring and minimize any real chance for interaction. In one, you're simply conducting an audition; in the other, you're spending half of the date not interacting at all.

My only real exception to this rule is for online dating; a low-investment date like coffee is more about a gut check than an actual date. You're testing how you feel about one another when you meet in the flesh... not to mention doing basic due diligence, trying to make sure that one or the other isn't a psycho axe-murdering cannibal.

Even so: a coffee date can be made to be more than just strangers asking questions while trying to pretend that the Starbucks they're drinking doesn't taste like burned ass. Pick a coffeehouse that does more than just coffee. Some double as music venues – while others even have improv and stand up comedy performances. Still more have board games, which can be a great ice breaker and allow for that competitive aspect that can get your juices flowing and the flirty trash-talking sparking.

An important, yet often neglected key to avoiding the awkward "interview" vibe on a first date is positioning. Think of your average job interview: you're staring nervously at your prospective employer who sits behind her massive desk as she asks the questions that decide your fate.

Now think about how you position yourself on a first date: sitting awkwardly across from one another at a table while you ask questions and hope you don't screw up. A simple change of where you're sitting – from directly across to perpendicular – completely changes the tone of the interaction. By sitting next to your date or at an angle, you remove the feeling that you're at odds with one another or the impression that there's a barrier between the two of you.

It feels much friendlier and less confrontational, which will put both of you at ease. It also – critically – makes it easier to engage in casual physical contact that would be awkward to attempt sitting face-to-face.

Your Date Is About The Two of You

I spend a fair amount of time out and about and eavesdropping on dates is a guilty pleasure of mine... which is why I'm continually astonished by the number of people who make this very basic mistake: they don't give their dates their full attention.

When you're on a date, you are there specifically to be with that other person, period. You are, presumably wanting to see how much you have in common and to have a good time... while generating a little of that all-important chemistry. Unfortunately, we live in a world full of distractions and constant interruptions that can be hard to tune out – especially if you're used to being wed to Twitter, Facebook or your email. Your date is about getting to know each other, not getting to know her AND checking up on your Facebook friends or the massive elbow strike that St. Pierre just landed on Diaz' jaw.

Which brings me to my point: turn off your motherfucking phone.

You wouldn't think that this needs to be said - and I'll be the first to admit I'm extremely bad about this - but far too many people blow a perfectly good first date by not cutting their electronic umbilical cord. I have personally seen far too many people on dates lose track of their conversation with their dates because they put their iPhones on the table and keep glancing at them every time a new email or text chimes in. Not only is it annoying to the people around you and poor etiquette in general but it's profoundly disrespectful to your date – you're explicitly telling her that she is not nearly as interesting as the latest update to your fantasy football league or whatever @PartyInMyPants69 had to say about that Buzzfeed article you just retweeted.

If you can't go more than 30 seconds without checking your phone, switch the damned thing off entirely. If you have some reason you absolutely must be reachable – a family member's medical emergency is acceptable (barely) – then set a filter; most smartphones have a "Do Not Disturb" function that will only allow specific numbers to ring through.

Other distractions can also ruin the flow of your date. Many bars – and some restaurants – have TVs; it can be hard to ignore these when they're constantly flickering in the corner of your eye. The obvious answer is to avoid dates at venues with TVs or projectors. However, if you find yourself at a place with televisions, turn yourself away from them. Get them completely out of your field of vision – I have seen far too many people get caught up in the TV behind their date rather than on the person sitting directly across from them. There's nothing more guaranteed to kill a wonderful date than when your date realizes you've only been paying half-attention to her because you're too caught up in the ESPN replays of last night's big game.

And believe me: your date will notice that you're distracted. And she will not appreciate it… which means that not only are you not getting a good-night kiss, never mind a second date, you're going to be lucky if she doesn't suddenly realize that she needs to go home and wash her cat.

Conversation Is Key

One of the surest signs that your date is going well when you both are so caught up in talking to each other that you lose track of time. The best dates often only end because you've realized that you're the only people left in the bar or restaurant and the staff has been getting increasingly unsubtle about stacking up the furniture and closing out for the night.

There's nothing quite as appealing as someone who can intrigue your mind as well as your squishy bits... and a bad conversationalist can kill any sexual interest deader than Christian Slater's career.

Fortunately, you don't need your own personal Cyrano DeBergerac whispering poetry in your ear to master conversation, you just need to follow some simple rules.

Ask Good Questions:
There's nothing worse than a date who will only talk about his favorite subject... especially when that subject is *him*. A date is about the two of you, which is why you want to make sure that you're showing interest in your date, and the best way you can do this is by asking questions. Questions are part of how we find commonalities and build rapport with one another... and they're how you keep from running into those awkward silences that leave you both feeling uncomfortable and scrambling to talk about something, *anything*.

Just don't be boring... those standard 10 First Date questions - "what do you do, where did you grow up" and so forth - will get you nowhere. Instead, ask your date about her hobbies and her passions. Pepper your conversation with a little naughtiness by the things the craziest thing she's ever done or what she would do if she had no chance of failure. If you need to get a conversation started, I always like to ask "Who was your favorite Bond girl?" or "Who was your favorite of the Doctor's companions?"

(Hint: the correct answer is either Martha Jones or Donna Noble. Just sayin')

Tell Stories:
When it's your turn to share about yourself, you want to have some stories to tell – that crazy night you and your friends crashed a VFW dance dressed in vintage fashions and learned how to swing with WWII vets[1], the epic road trip you took with your friends or even just the wacky things that happen on a daily basis. As I mentioned in the chapter about building chemistry, the basics of a good story are simple: you want to keep them relatively short, vivid and should have an ending that provokes a "awww", "cool!" or a laugh. Help bring them to life by creating characters; use voices, change your posture, anything to make them more distinct These stories are chance to subtly brag about yourself and let your date know what a relationship with you might be like... so you want to paint as attractive a picture as possible.

(Obviously, if you don't have stories to tell... well, really, you need to go out and start collecting them!)

Avoid Negativity
Negativity has no place on a date. Negativity is the emotional black hole from which attraction and fun cannot escape. This means no moaning or complaining about your job, your friends, your life, the restaurant or anything else. If your job sucks, don't talk about it. Just say "yeah, it's just something to pay the bills for now" and change the subject. Complaining about your friends will just make your date wonder why the hell they're in your life in the first place. It's hard to have fun when the other person is relentlessly negative – and fun should be your goal. If you have nothing positive to say about a particular topic, change the subject and move on.

This goes doubly so for your exes. I don't necessarily subscribe to the "no talking about your exes" rule, but you definitely do not want to talk shit about them. All complaining about an ex does is tell your date how you're going to talk about him if/when the two of you don't work out... and the last thing you need to do is plant that idea in his head.

Remember: this doesn't mean that the only things you can talk about are your successes. If you have a story of some epic screw-up that you can tell in a way that's funny and engaging - rather than depressing - then by all means, tell it. I'll cheerfully tell stories where I've done dumb shit or that don't paint me in the best light - The Midnight Toilet Frog What Leaps At Midnight, for example, is all about my freaking out during a camping trip - because they're good for a laugh. Being able to laugh at yourself is always a plus. Just make sure you don't rely on self-deprecating humor. There's a fine line between being willing to laugh at yourself and apologizing for being you.

Dial Back The Booze and Chill

Yes, first dates can be nerve-wracking endurance-fests where you feel like you're walking through an emotional minefield and any wrong step is going to blow away your chance of getting blown later.... But you need to be able to relax. However, trying to help that along with Scotch can actually end up backfiring.

First dates and alcohol go together like Japanese school-girls and giant robots – they seem like a natural fit, but the potential for trouble often outweighs the benefits. It's natural to want to have a drink or two on a date – a beer to ease those jittery nerves, a second to act as a social lubricant, a third because you're pretty sure the first got lost on the way to your stomach and you need to send out a search party – but it's entirely too easy to lose track and end up with problems you could have otherwise avoided. The line between a pleasant buzz and "removing a much-needed mental filter" is thin indeed, and you don't want to end up tripping over your own dick because the whiskey convinced you that jokes about anal sex mishaps were a good idea.

Similarly, you don't want to give the impression that you're trying to get your date a little drunk; the idea that you're plying her with alcohol will send up the "creeper" vibe faster than just about anything else you can do, even if your intentions are perfectly honorable.

This isn't to say that you should avoid alcohol entirely - just keep it to one or two before switching to water or soda. Drinking to ease your nerves can seem like a good idea at first, but it can rapidly descend into a morass of bad decisions.

Remember: the key to a great first date is to have fun... and if you're so caught up with anxiety and stress that you could vibrate through space and time, that's just not going to happen.

Part of the reason for these nerves is the self-imposed pressure to make a good impression. Some people get so concerned with the idea of impressing their date that they end up going much further than they need to – expensive dinners, hard-to-get tickets to shows, large bouquets of flowers... It's nice if you can afford it, but sometimes not only is it a case of diminishing returns but sometimes you end up with the opposite effect and scare your date off. Frankly, less is often more; a fun night of bowling and a couple Miller Lights is going to go better than an uncomfortable dinner at a gourmet restaurant with a bottle of Veuve Clicquot.

Moreover, trying to impress your date with how much money you have is a bad idea; not only are you communicating that you think her affections can be bought but you're inadvertently sending the message that you're expecting equal compensation for how much you're spending.

But just as important as not trying to go over the top to impress your date is to not put so much pressure on yourself that you can't actually enjoy the date itself. If you're so keyed up about making everything go perfectly, you're going to end up a twitchy bundle of nerves... and that's going to make your date uncomfortable, too. Frankly, the best attitude you can adopt is one of "No big deal". Dating disasters – spilled drinks, inconvenient stains, spoiled plans – suck, but being able to handle them with aplomb, grace and a sense of humor will not only get you past them but will actually make your date that much more memorable and charming. Being able to take a mistake in stride and good cheer makes it much easier to recover, and that recovery will say more for you and your sense of confidence than anything else you do... and that will impress your date.

And you can't do that when you're buzzed.

Even in the worst moments of awkwardness, be willing to face it head on. Nothing kills the awkward faster than calling it out. Acknowledging that yes, things might be a little uncomfortable or that you're a touch nervous isn't a sign of weakness, it's a sign of strength - you're confident enough to be honest with your date instead of trying to put up a false front. Plus, it's almost guaranteed that she's feeling just as nervous as you are; being the one to call it out will make her feel better and help release all that pressure.

Go For The Kiss

Whether to kiss on the first date or not is often a matter of contentious debate and personal preference. Some people resolutely won't, while others have no problem burning up the sheets if the date goes well enough.

Personally, I'm a fan of kissing *before* the end of the date, but that's me; if you're not confident in your ability to read the signs that she wants you to kiss her, then it's not going to hurt if you wait until the end of the evening. I am of the firm opinion that, absent a clear wave-off, it's worth at least making the attempt... provided you're classy about it. If you don't - especially if you haven't been 100% clear from the beginning that the two of you are on a date - you run the risk of being too timid and possibly inadvertently signaling that you're not interested in her sexually. So, as you walk your date back to the car or to their door, pause. Tell her what a good time you had that night... then lean in slowly. Give her the option of giving you the cheek – or even a complete wave-off – if that's what she wants. When you do kiss her, keep it light – which means no tongue - and just the once. If she wants you to kiss her again, she'll almost certainly let you know in no uncertain terms. Let your date take the lead in how intense to go – better to hold back a little than to inadvertently maul them instead.

If you do get the cheek, then you act as though that's exactly what you intended to do. Don't call attention to it – that doesn't help. Accept that she's not ready to kiss you this time and you will have far better odds of there being a next time. Acting like a cock about it or trying for the kiss anyway is only going to guarantee that there will be no second date.

Ever.

---

[1] Also a true story.

TWELVE

STOP OVER-THINKING IT

Catching The Ball - Or: Stop Overthinking It

I often compare dating to catching a ball that's been tossed to you. You watch the ball, you reach up, catch it, maybe through it back. Easy-peasy, right?

Except when you think about it... it's really not. You're doing *insanely* high level math *in nanoseconds, in your goddamn head.* You're having to calculate the trajectory of the ball, measure it's velocity, factor in wind resistance, the parabola of its falling arc relative to *your* position, *all in 3D space.*

Next, you have to gauge your own reaction time relative to the ball's presumed target and move fast enough so as to position yourself to catch the ball, extend your arm in 3D space precisely so as to catch it without injuring yourself or swatting the ball out of the way instead.

Congratulations. You have just done something that engineers at NASA require super-computers for whenever they want to dock the Shuttle with the International Space Station or repair an orbiting satellite... and *you're doing it without even thinking consciously.*

Then, just to make matters even *more* complicated, you have to do every single one of those calculations *again,* except this time *in reverse*, when you throw the ball *back* to the person who tossed it to you in the first place.

What takes thousands of man-hours and petaflops of computing power to calculate, you've accomplished in the span of seconds.

The same sorts of processes apply just to standing up and walking a few steps - you're constantly gauging the necessary level of force to lift a specific mass (your body) while simultaneously adjusting your balance and weight distribution in order to maintain your balance as you shift your center of gravity from your chair to over your feet. *Then* you're having to calculate the distance between your current location and your destination while adjusting the position of two independently moving, multi-jointed levers in 3D space while simultaneously making thousands of micro adjustments in order to keep you from falling over while constantly measuring the relationship of force and the friction necessary to overcome inertia in order to propel you forward..

Think all of that's easy? Look at how long it's taken scientists to come up with a bipedal robot capable of walking on it's own; they haven't gotten so far as getting one that can walk up and down *stairs*, something *you* mastered as an *infant*.

But when you start thinking about all the complexities involved... suddenly you can't do it anymore.

Ever want to screw up somebody's putt on the golf-course? Ask them if they inhale on the backswing; they'll suddenly be so conscious of everything they do that they won't be able to actually complete a simple putt... even if it's something that they've done a thousand times before. This is known as "The Centipede's Dilemma"- the centipede had no problems walking until someone asked it how it keeps all of those legs straight.

The moment you start over-thinking something is the moment you find that you can't do it.

In psychology, there are four stages of competence when you're learning a new skill: Unconscious Incompetence, Conscious Incompetence, Conscious Competence and Unconscious Competence. That is, you're unaware of what it takes to do something, you're aware that you can't do it, you know what you need to do but you have to think it through, and then, finally, being able to do something as naturally as breathing.

To take it back to an earlier example, think of walking. We don't think about everything it takes to walk – the constantly shifting our balance, spacing our feet etc. - because we have achieved unconscious competence. As infants, though we started off unaware that walking was even a *thing*; we barely had gross motor skills down. But then we started to realize that walking was something we wanted to do... but we didn't know how. Through practice – pulling ourselves up on things, taking those first few stumbling steps, we started to *learn* through trial and error. Before too long, we start being able to walk like it ain't no thing and it becomes a part of our muscle memory. But when you try to intellectualize the process, it makes you all the more conscious of what you're doing and thus overwhelms you.

Thus the problem with overthinking. By letting ourselves become overly-conscious about that putt, that footstep, catching that ball or going on that date, you're moving *backwards* in the skill states.

Does She Like Me? or: Wishful (Over)Thinking

We tend to overthink things that we're emotionally

invested in. Let's take an obvious example of overthinking: the eternal question of "Does She Like Me?"

It summons up the image of one's junior-high days, when the eternal question was "does she like me, or does she *like* me?" and the confusing morass of social codes and the need to uphold a certain image; after all, it wouldn't do to just ask, now would it?

And for all of the associations with immaturity and social inexperience, guys often let themselves get caught up in a never-ending spiral of questioning their instincts and impulses when it comes to whether somebody is genuinely interested in them or not. They will try to read meaning into every gesture and micro-expression and find signals in the tonality of her voice and the tilt of her head when she asks "So how was your weekend?" The slight inflection on the "your", the twitch of her eye-lid... is this a sign that she's trying to see if you're still single? If you say that you spent the weekend with friends, is she going to assume they were all guys, or that maybe there's a woman in the mix? Or what if she's just taunting you, letting you know that she knows you couldn't possibly bring the level of excitement that she's used to?

Or perhaps she's just making polite small-talk and means exactly what she said.

When you're socially inexperienced, trying to read a woman's signals can be a challenge; you feel as though you're always walking the line between assuming that everything she's saying is exactly what she means and the possibility that there's an underlying message that you're not quite understanding. It also doesn't help that men and women are socialized to communicate differently. Men are encouraged to be forward, even aggressive, in their interactions with others; the idea that somebody is upfront and honest is often a mark of pride and seen as a testament to their integrity and character. Women, on the other hand, have been socialized to be indirect - to be overly considerate to the feelings of others, even prioritizing them over their own. So while men will often say exactly what they mean, women are taught to couch their preferences or meaning in softer terms in order to avoid causing offense. Men are taught to say "no"; women are taught to refuse politely and indirectly. A woman, for example might turn down being asked out on a date with "I'm not looking to date anyone right now..." as a way of softening the blow. But while she means "I'm not interested in you", men hear "...but I might be ready to date later."

But while guys might be forgiven for occasionally mistaking a polite refusal for a deferred "yes", the fact of the matter is, the main reason for the confusion is that they're hoping for the answer they want even in the face of reality. This is why guys often fall victim to overthinking and overanalyzing the possibility of a woman's interest: they're looking for looking for signs that what they want is what's going on, even when they ultimately know the real answer.

When you're emotionally invested in the outcome of the interaction - getting her to date you, say - then it's all too easy to let your desire lead you to false positives. Men who find themselves in the so-called Friend Zone will often spend time poring over everything a woman says or does in hopes of finding signs that she's starting to return their feelings. But what they're really doing is looking for reasons to keep the fantasy alive. The fact that she left her hand on your shoulder a microsecond longer than she did a week ago isn't a sign that perhaps she's warming up to you, it's a coincidence. Over-thinking every interaction, trying to find the hidden meanings, is just a way avoid the uncomfortable truth: you know she's not interested in you and likely never will be.

Most nonverbal communication is actually very easy to read; the confusion only crops up when you're longing for a "correct" answer. If you're reading the metaphorical tea-leaves in an attempt to figure out how someone is feeling, then you already have your answer... you just don't want to hear it.

Over-Analysis, Anxiety and the Illusion of Progress

We over-think it because it's easier to let our brains run around in circles than to actually face the emotional underpinnings of the problem. Men are taught to be disassociated from our emotions - even in this day and age, expressing ourselves openly and honestly about our feelings isn't considered "manly" - and it's easier to try to intellectualize a problem than to process how we're feeling about it.

The insidious part about over-thinking is that it feels like we're actually getting somewhere. We're spending a lot of brain-cycles analyzing the issue, looking for evidence, coming up with potential explanations, rejecting them, finding new explanations, drafting plans... all of which creates the illusion that we're making progress when in reality, we're actually causing ourselves to lock up and not do anything.

It's a form of procrastination disguised as busy-work, the mental equivalent of what I call cat-hoovering. You have something you need to do - write a paper, pay bills, something that you would rather avoid. At the same time, however, you know that just doing nothing will only make it weigh heavier on your mind, so you find a way to give you the impression that you're actually being productive without getting any closer to actually accomplishing the task at hand. So rather than simply sitting down and getting it done, you find excuses as to why you can't do it right now, things you need to do before you can do the project. You can't write your paper just yet because your desk is a mess; all that clutter is distracting, so you need to clean up and reorganize everything. An orderly environment is a productive environment, after all. So you clean off your desk and organize your papers... but then you realize that the rest of the room is just as disordered, so you proceed to give it the long-overdue deep cleaning it deserves.

Before too long you find that you've cleaned the entire house and are rapidly running out of distractions to the point you are considering vacuuming the cat rather than actually doing the work.

Thus: cat-hoovering.

Over-thinking follows the same pattern. You have a motivating desire that could be potentially unpleasant, emotionally; therefore you find ways of avoiding it that feel like you're confronting it.

Approach anxiety from Chapter 6, for example, is a classic case of over-thinking as a way to avoid an emotionally uncomfortable situation. There is the motivating desire -to approach someone we're attracted to - followed by the fear of being rejected. We don't want to feel that fear - even more than we want to avoid the actual pain of the rejection - and so we intellectualize the problem. We come up with rationalizations as to why we couldn't possibly approach her now and start to make plans on how we could go and introduce ourselves. But then we immediately reject those plans because of any number of imagined worst-case scenarios and end up drafting new plans that turn out to be equally as flawed.

It feels like we're working our way through the approach anxiety when in reality, we're ensuring that our feet remain firmly rooted to the floor. We've successfully avoided that emotional discomfort by tricking ourselves into thinking that we're confronting it. We are, essentially going nowhere as fast as we possibly can.

The great irony, of course, is that by devoting so much time to avoiding the discomfort, we end up making it worse. We take things that are simple, that we can do easily and render ourselves incapable - moving backwards along the states of competence.

Think of all the times you've gotten yourself worked up over talking to somebody you were attracted to. You talk to people every day without sounding like a stammering idiot, so why do you freak out when it's something important? It's because you're emotionally invested in the outcome and thus are afraid of failing. You're hoping to convince Sarah, the hot photographer you met at Starbucks, to go on a date with you and you're afraid of her shooting you down. You become hyper-aware of every single twitch of her face and her body language because you're desperately trying to work through your discomfort without actually confronting it. Instead of stopping, taking a deep breath and slowing your roll, you're babbling on like a moron who just can't stop talking and saying stupider and stupider things as you try to backpedal and change the subject. Before you know it, you've spent five minutes rambling around the possibility of a date without actually having made a lick of sense and Sarah is wondering what the hell just happened.

So what do we do?

Own Your Emotions

The key to avoiding over-thinking is to stop, take stock of what you're doing and - critically - be willing to face your discomfort.

Whenever I've started to freak out over whether or not I'd somehow blown my chance with a woman I was into - to pick a random example -, I've had to *force* myself to calm down. Take a deep breath; breathe in for the count of five, hold it for the count of three, then breathe out for the count of ten. The act of controlling your breathing *forces* your heart to slow down and reduces the physical effects of your anxiety. From there it became a matter of adjustment of my expectations.

The first step is to recognize that you're over-thinking things - critically, without starting to over-thinking the possibility that you're over-thinking. The easiest way to tell is to examine just what you've *actually done* about the issue at hand: have you taken concrete action or have you convinced yourself you need to keep working to find a solution? The more that you're finding reasons to *not* do something, the more you're over-thinking an issue.

The next is to acknowledge and face the fact that you're trying to *avoid* the issue. In my case, I'd be looking for proof that I *hadn't* screwed up by over-analyzing every single thing I'd said, followed by combing through her social networks for any evidence that I *had*... the constant questioning, searching and analyzing was my way of avoiding the heart of the matter: that I was afraid of being rejected. Part of facing it meant that I had to face up to the fact that it *may well have happened*; I tripped over my own dick, came across as too pushy or too eager or otherwise boorish and alienated her. I had to accept it and be willing to just move on.

The key is to cultivate an abundance mentality. When you're coming from a place of scarcity, *every* failure reinforces the underlying fear and anxiety that you're trying to avoid by making them a matter of apocalyptic importance. When you accept that there are millions, if not *billions* of sexually available women in the world, you start to realize that one screw up is just that: a blip in the system, a glitch in The Matrix. You messed up with one person; now you'll do better the next time. Rejection still *hurts*, but it doesn't become a referendum on your worth as an individual or another step on the way to eternal loneliness before giving up and longing for the sweet embrace of oblivion. It's simply another growing pain along the path to improvement.

It also helps to externalize your emotions; you acknowledge that you *feel* them instead of that you *are* them. I had to remind myself that I *felt* afraid that I might've gotten dumped, not that I *was* afraid; the fear was an *emotion* I was experiencing, not a state of being. And in the spirit of emotional honesty, I also had to recognize: as unpleasant as it was, the world hadn't ended. I wasn't *happy*, but the world hadn't come crashing down around my ears. The sun still rose and set and life went on.

From there, the next step is simply to take responsibility, both for your actions and your response to it. I may very well have pissed her off; I had to be willing to acknowledge my part and not just dismiss it as inherently unfair or her being unreasonable. It resulted in my being rejected and now I had a choice: I could cowboy up or I could lay there and bleed. I could cry and whinge and moan or I could *learn* from it.

The more you learn to own your own emotions, to be willing to confront those discomforts and fears, the less you will find yourself prone to over-thinking and over-analysis... and you'll find that dating becomes *much* simpler.

Part Four:

The Simplified Dating Mindset

Thirteen

The Three "Be"s

Wu Wei or: Let The Force Flow Through You

The last thing I want to leave you with is the importance of a proper mindset.

Simplifying dating is about more than just a matter of skills - it's about acceptance. In many ways, we end up being our own worst enemies; we get so absorbed in what we want that we end up making things worse.

Like most nerds of my generation, I grew up loving Star Wars, especially the idea of the Force. Who wouldn't fall in love with the idea of learning how to be a super-powered, telekinetic ninja? But it was the philosophy that fascinated me the most; the idea that you were supposed to just do rather than try, to let things flow rather than to direct them... how were you supposed to ever make anything happen that way? But if it was working for Yoda, maybe there was something to it.

Later on in life, I learned that George Lucas cribbed most of his ideas from the concept of the Tao; in fact, Star Wars remains possibly the best way to describe the Tao itself. One of the central tenets of Taoism is the concept of the wu wei or "action without action". A tree, for example, doesn't try to grow, it just grows. By the same token, you don't want to try to date, you want to just date. You want to practice action without excess effort.

Or to put it another way: you want to let go and let the Force flow through you instead of trying to direct it. Instead of struggling and suffering, you want to relax and live in a way that lets dating be simpler and more natural.

Of course, this is easier said than done. Anyone who's struggled with dating isn't going to buy into the idea that dating is just something that you do without thinking about it. And therein lies the problem. We get so caught up in the process and our anxieties that dating becomes a struggle. It's no longer something enjoyable, a way to meet people and form some connections, maybe even some naked connections. It's a trial. It's a judgement on everything about us. It's a competition between us and anyone else who's ever dated this person before... or may date her afterwards.

How the hell is anybody supposed to *enjoy* that?

This is why I believe in what I call the Three "Be"s. These are the cornerstone of the mindset I believe in for being able to simply date.

Be Imperfect

If there is one area where most people seem to screw themselves over in dating, it's that they let themselves obsess about everything. When you hear "obsession", the mind often jumps to Oneitis - the idea that this person we're attracted to is our One True Soul Mate and nobody else in the world will ever be as amazing or perfect or otherwise just The One. Yes, getting hung up on the belief that this person or that person or some other person is The One is going to hold you back in dating. However, it's more than just about any particular individual. This tendency to obsess shows up in all aspects of dating.

I have lost track of how many people have written to me in a panic, believing that some little detail has totally derailed their date or destroyed their relationship. They beat themselves up over the fact that they weren't absolutely perfect on their first, second or even third date with their particular snugglebunny. They become so focused on the end goal that they believe that anything other than getting 100% is going to condemn them to failure.

Except… that's not how dating works.

It's a common misconception that dating is somehow a competition against every person your date has ever gone out with. If you don't somehow outshine the studliest of the Dirk Chestmeats in her life, then you're doomed to be given the dreaded Let's Just Be Friends speech and be sent back home alone to cry and masturbate to increasingly fucked up porn, using your tears as lube.

Here's the shocking secret: you're not in competition with anybody. Yeah, everybody has a past. Everybody has people they've dated before you and some of them may or may not be handsomer, richer, taller, better in bed or just all-around better than you in some way shape or form. But your date isn't with them right now. She's here. With you. And all you need to do is just be good enough.

It's remarkably liberating when you realize that you don't need to beat out everybody else. All you have to do is be the person she wants to be with. The one who makes her feel amazing. The one who gets her on a level nobody else does. The one who makes her laugh. You may not be her 100% perfect man, but that's ok. She's not the 100% perfect woman either.

Perfection is for pianos, where the slightest flaw or miscalibration can ruin the whole instrument. You're not dating a piano, you're dating a person who is just as flawed and fucked up as you are. When you let perfection become the enemy of the good, you end up sabotaging your own progress. Your expectations make things harder.

When you're convinced that you're just one ill-timed sneeze or bad joke away from having your date bail out on you like Maverick ejecting from an F-15, you're not going to have fun. That, in turn is going to reflect in your behavior – you're going to be tense and nervous, uptight and hyper-aware of everything. You're going to make your date tense and uncomfortable because you're tense and uncomfortable and this can rapidly become an inescapable downward spiral of suck.

So stop worrying about perfection. Embrace that things are going to go wrong or get weird. You're probably going to fart a little too audibly. But that's ok because your date is likely going to snort when she laughs or accidentally fling her appetizer across the room. You're going to make a joke that falls flat, your date will inadvertently make a sexual innuendo that's going to sound incredibly obscene and then the waiter is going to bring the wrong entree and both of you are going to have the embarrassing question of "Do you send it back and risk looking high-maintenance or do you just eat something you really didn't want?"

The key is just to accept that it happened and move on instead of dwelling on it or letting something stupid define the rest of your evening. Here's your mantra: if you don't treat it like a big deal, they won't treat it like a big deal. Shrug, blush a little, move on. There are more important things to worry about.

Even if you're dating Kerry Washington or Christina Hendricks or Taylor Swift, you don't have to be some hero from a cheesy romance novel come to sweep her off her feet and take her on a night that she's never known. All that you need is for the two of you to have fun together. If she enjoys hanging out with you and the way that she feels when she's with you, she's going to want to see you again... even if you spent the last ten minutes with a piece of spinach wedged between your teeth.

Be Outcome Independent

Don't get hung up on the outcome.

This can seem a little counter-intuitive; after all, the whole point of dating is the outcome, no? You're presumably dating this person because you're looking for a relationship; that is inherently the exact opposite of being outcome independent.

But then, focusing on that outcome is often the problem in the first place. The idea that "you find love when you're not looking for it" is one of the most annoying non-answers in advice-giving, because it's so goddamn vague and smugly unhelpful. It sounds like it's saying one thing – stop trying and then let Fate/God/The Force/whatever do the work for you – but what it's really saying is that you shouldn't get so hung up on the end goal that you let it overwhelm everything else in dating… including actually connecting with the person you're on a date with.

Dating with an end-goal in mind ends up being a living incarnation of Xeno's Paradox; you're always moving forward, but ultimately you're not getting any closer to where you want to be.

It's better instead to enjoy the journey rather than constantly trying to see whether or not you're any closer to your goal, whether that goal is finding your One True Love[1], or trying to get more sex. It's a great way to psych yourself out; if you treat each date as your only shot at the big money, you're setting yourself up with overwhelming expectations that only end up disappointing you. It plays into the scarcity mentality that insists that each "failed" date (for suitably personal definitions of failure) is one step closer to being Forever Alone.

Even when you're just putting all of your emphasis on a smaller goal like "getting a second date", this not only puts an incredible amount of pressure on you – and your date -

but you end up focusing on "What do I have to do to get you to go out with me again?" instead of "who is this person and what's cool about them?"

When you're outcome independent – when you don't worry about how the night is going to end – then you're actually free to enjoy yourself. You can spend less time worrying about whether there's a chance at a second date or getting laid tonight or if you're doing X, Y or Z right, and more time just enjoying your time together. Your goal shouldn't be about trying to figure out whether or not you're talking to your future spouse (or your future 10 minutes of squishy noises and post-coital cigarettes), it should just be on connecting with them and getting to know them. Let the date be the end goal in and of itself. Flirt just because flirting is fun. Tell stories not because you're trying to show that you're long-term relationship material but because sometimes cool shit happens and it's fun to share that with other people.

It's part of having an abundance mentality; when you know that there will be others, you're not so invested in the outcome. When you're not invested in the outcome, you're free to relax and take things as they come. You're not uptight and anxious. You won't over-think every word that comes out of your mouth or every moment of the date. You can let yourself relax and just be.

If things go well, then great! If the date doesn't lead anywhere… that's ok. You still met someone cool and had a good time, maybe even learned a little about yourself that can help you later on. Don't beat yourself up that you didn't "get" the girl – whether for sex, another date, or a steady relationship – because hey, you weren't trying to "get" anything. You met up with someone, you had some drinks and a couple laughs.

That sounds like a pretty good night to me.

Be Present

A word about time. Most people assume that time is linear when in reality it's a little more wibbly-wobbly....stuff.

Sorry. The reference got away from me for a second there. Ahem.

More to the point: the past is over and the future never comes. We are only ever in the "now".

But so few of us live in the "now". We spend too much time hung up in the past and letting it bleed into our present, or sacrificing our present in the name of some imagined future that may never happen.

Confused? Stick with me for a moment.

We rarely let the past just be the past. We latch on to it and keep it with us at all times. We hold on to it, we replay it over and over again, we castigate ourselves for it and sometimes we try to edit it into what we really wanted to happen.

Because we hold on to the past so tightly, we let it color our present. We don't learn from it, mind you; we just drag our old traumas, fears and regrets around with us in our day to day lives like a neurotic security blanket, letting them inform everything we do. Screwed up in the past? If you let those old mistakes define you, then you can never let yourself grow and improve as a person. Had a bad experience with a woman in the past? If you let that experience be the barometer for every interaction you have with a woman from that point on, you're cheating yourself out of some of the greatest times of your life, simply because you don't want to let a wound close and fade away.

I should know. I lost several relationships because I kept holding on to old hurts, letting them haunt me like ghosts. I had a bad experience and spent every subsequent relationship always on the lookout for a repeat... which would inevitably happen because focusing on the past is a damn good way to make it repeat itself. I couldn't enjoy myself in the moment because I was too afraid of what had happened before. I kept waiting for that shoe to drop and when it did – because my focus on it affected my behavior which in turn affected my girlfriend's behavior – it only reinforced my obsession with that past fear.

It could be anything: a girlfriend who lied to you and cheated on you. Your old identity as a dateless loser, lurking just under the surface, daring everyone around you to see it and call you a fraud. A girl who broke your heart because she didn't love you the way you loved her. Anything. Carrying those fossilized hurts and spectral fears with you doesn't help; it only ever keeps you from appreciating what you have now.

Similarly, obsessing about the future takes you away from the present. It's an extension of being outcome independent; being overly focused on the future, whether it's the next date or the rest of your lives together, leaves you unable to enjoy the present. One of my best friends can't do anything without anticipating every possible thing that's going to metaphorically bite her in the ass. She likes to "borrow" trouble, even when there isn't any to be had. Small wonder, then, that most of her relationships are short and turbulent; when you're always expecting problems, you'll inevitably find them.

You need to focus on the "now". You can learn from your past mistakes – the better not to make them again – but let go of them when you do. You can hope for the future, even invest in it, but you need to be willing to let the future take care of itself. There is no profit in borrowing trouble; getting lost in a cascading spiral of what-ifs only serves to make you over-think everything and sacrifices your ability to just be.

When you're focused on being present, you're able to enjoy things as they are. You don't let yourself worry about all the myriad ways that you've done things wrong before. You don't obsess about what's going to happen next. You just let yourself be in the moment, taking things as they come. Later on you can do the post-game analysis and figure out how to do things better.

For right now though: There is no future. There is no past. There is only this moment right here, right now and you're missing it.

---

[1] There *is* no One.

FOURTEEN

THE END OF THE BEGINNING

It's A Gift To Be Simple

I've got a tattoo on my forearm from the I-Ching. It's the 63rd hexagram, "After Completion". I got it as a reminder that there is always more; you are never finished learning, never finished growing. Even when an equilibrium has been reached, its always possible to fall back into disorder.

It's also the mark of the Arashikage ninja clan from G.I. Joe, but that's another matter, pay it no mind. I'm philosophizing here. Pay attention, this is deep stuff.

The point is that simplifying dating - stripping out the excesses, focusing on the important aspects and learning to avoid the pitfalls - is an ongoing process. There is no "end" to it, any more than there's an end in an ongoing relationship; it continues until it is no longer there. There isn't a point where you will be able to say "there we go; I've done it. I have mastered dating." There will always be more to work on, more things that you could improve upon. There will be parts that come naturally to you and parts that you will struggle with all of your life.

There's a reason why I call this book *Simplified* Dating, not *Easy* Dating. Just because you've simplified something doesn't mean you've made it easy; it just means you've made it more efficient. It means you're trying to let it flow and be enjoyable rather than trying to fight against it. You still have much to learn and much to do.

And that's OK.

Hell, that's more than OK. That's brilliant. Because dating, whether it's with one person or many, whether serious or casual, should be an ongoing process. The instant that you feel you have no more to learn from or about your partner, that she has no more to offer and you have nothing else to talk about, is the instant your relationship has ended.

And then you start over again. Equilibrium had been reached, and you've fallen back into disorder. Time to strive again.

Good luck.

About The Author

Harris O'Malley (AKA Dr. NerdLove) is an Austin-based, internationally recognized blogger and dating coach who provides geek dating advice at Paging Dr. NerdLove and his bi-weekly advice column "Ask Dr. NerdLove" on Kotaku.

O'Malley been featured in The Guardian, The Washington Post, The Austin-American Statesman, New York Magazine Think Progress, Lifehacker, Wired, Buzzfeed, Huffington Post Live, Sex Nerd Sandra, The Art of Charm, Sex With Timaree, Daily Life, Slate, MTV's Guy Code, Boing Boing and The Harvard Business Journal. He has been named one of the top 10 geek dating blogs by DatingAdvice.com.

For more more advice on dating, sex & relationships, visit him online at www.doctornerdlove.com

Keep up with the latest from Dr. NerdLove:
twitter.com/DrNerdLove
facebook.com/DrNerdLove
doc@doctornerdlove.com

81742085R00081

Made in the USA
Lexington, KY
20 February 2018